GOD'S WISDOM
AND POWER

THE STORY BIBLE SERIES

1. *God's Family* tells the story of creation, God's promises to Abraham's family, and the adventures of Joseph.

2. *God Rescues His People* tells about Israel's escape from Egypt, Moses and the Ten Commandments, and the wandering in the wilderness.

3. *God Gives the Land* tells the story of Joshua, the adventures of the judges, and the story of Ruth.

4. *God's Chosen King* tells about Samuel, Saul, and David, God's promises to David's family, and the Psalms.

5. *God's Wisdom and Power* tells about the glorious reign of Solomon, the wonderful works of Elijah and Elisha, and the Proverbs and the Song of Songs.

Additional books in the series will tell stories from the rest of the Old Testament and from the New Testament.

Story Bible Series, Book 5

GOD'S WISDOM AND POWER

Stories of God and His People: 1 and 2 Kings, 2 Chronicles, Proverbs, and the Song of Songs

Retold by Eve B. MacMaster
Illustrated by James Converse

HERALD PRESS
Scottdale, Pennsylvania
Kitchener, Ontario
1984

Library of Congress Cataloging in Publication Data

MacMaster, Eve, 1942-
  God's wisdom and power.

  (Story Bible series; bk. 5)
  Summary: Presents the Old Testament stories about
Solomon, Elijah, and Elisha. Includes maps of the king-
doms and empires of the known world of the period.
    1. Bible stories, English—O.T. [1. Bible stories—
O.T.] I. Converse, James, ill. II. Title. III. Series.
BS551.2M297 1984   221.9'505   84-8974
ISBN 0-8361-3362-5 (pbk.)

The Story of This Book

Several years ago I was looking for a Bible story book to read to my children. I wanted one that was complete, without tacked-on morals or a denominational interpretation. I wanted one that was faithful to the Bible and fun to read. I couldn't find what I was looking for.

With the encouragement of my husband, Richard Mac-Master, I approached Herald Press with the idea of the series: a retelling of the whole Bible with nothing added and nothing subtracted, just following the story line through the Old and New Testaments.

The people at Herald Press were agreeable and enthusiastic and gave much valuable advice, especially book editor Paul M. Schrock.

At his suggestion, I asked some academic and professional people in our community to check the stories for style and accuracy. This advisory committee, who have kindly volunteered their time, includes Bible professors George R. Brunk III, Ronald D. Guengerich, G. Irvin Lehman, and Kenneth Seitz; childhood curriculum and librarian specialists Elsie G. Lehman and A. Arlene Bumbaugh; and book marketing specialist Angie B. Williams.

I hope this series will lead its readers to the original, for no retelling is a substitute for the Bible itself. The Bible is actually a collection of books written over a long period of time in a variety of forms. It has been translated and retold in every generation, because people everywhere want to know what God is like.

The main character in every story is God. The plot of every story is God's activity among his people: creating, saving, fighting, reigning, and doing works of wisdom and power.

The first book in the series is *God's Family*. It tells stories about God the Creator.

The second book is *God Rescues His People*. It tells stories about God the Savior.

The third book is *God Gives the Land*. It tells stories about God the warrior.

The fourth book, *God's Chosen King*, tells stories about God the true King.

This book, *God's Wisdom and Power*, tells stories about God, the source of wisdom and power.

This volume is dedicated to my friend Ruth Brunk Stoltzfus, whose life is a witness to the wisdom and power of God.

—Eve MacMaster
Bridgewater, Virginia
Epiphany, 1984

Contents

Stories About Solomon

Plots in the Palace

1 Kings 1

JERUSALEM was buzzing with rumors. Who was going to be the next king of Israel? Nobody knew for sure. Some thought King David would choose Adonijah, his eldest living son. Others said David would pick Solomon. David had many sons to choose from.

The Lord God of Israel had blessed David with many wives and children. He had given David victory on the battlefield, wealth, power, and success. The Lord loved David so much, he promised that one of David's descendants would always rule over Israel.

Now David was old and feeble, and it was time for him to choose which of his sons would become the next king. When would he announce his decision?

Adonijah was tired of waiting. He bought some horses and chariots and hired fifty men to run ahead of him as he drove through Jerusalem. Everyone in the city noticed the handsome young prince; he looked like a king already.

Some of David's high officials agreed to work with Adonijah and help him become king. Among them were Joab, the commander of David's army, and Abiathar, the high priest.

But some other men had a different idea. They plotted against Adonijah and his supporters. Benaiah, the captain of the palace guard, and Zadok the priest worked with Nathan the prophet to make Solomon king.

Then Adonijah arranged a great feast at En-rogel, a spring in the Kidron Valley, just outside the walls of Jerusalem. He invited all the royal princes except Solomon, and all the high officials except Captain Benaiah, Zadok the priest, and Nathan the prophet.

While Adonijah and his guests were celebrating at En-rogel, Nathan went to see Bathsheba, the mother of Solomon.

"Have you heard what's going on?" he asked her. "David doesn't know it, but Haggith's son Adonijah is making himself king!"

Haggith was another one of David's many wives.

Since they had the same father, but different mothers, Adonijah and Solomon were half brothers.

"Listen to my advice," said Nathan. "Go see David right now. I'll tell you what to say, and when you're finished, I'll come in and say the same thing."

Bathsheba followed Nathan's advice. She went to David's room, where she found him lying in bed. His youngest wife, the beautiful Abishag, was waiting on him.

"What do you want?" asked David.

"My lord," answered Bathsheba, bowing low, "you made a solemn promise in the name of the Lord your God that my son Solomon would become king after you. You said, 'He is the one who will sit on my throne.'

"But now Adonijah is making himself king! He

has invited all the princes except Solomon to feast with him and Commander Joab and Abiathar the priest. Everyone in Israel is waiting to find out what you're going to do about it.

"If you don't do something right away, Adonijah will be the next king. And then what will happen to me and your son Solomon? Our lives will be in danger!"

While Bathsheba was still speaking, Nathan entered David's room. Bathsheba excused herself.

"My lord king," said Nathan with a bow. "Have you really announced that Adonijah will be the next king? He's down at En-rogel now, celebrating with his friends. They're all shouting, 'Long live King Adonijah!' Joab and Abiathar and the royal princes are there, but Benaiah and Zadok and I and Solomon weren't invited. Is this what you want? Have you given them your approval?"

"Call Bathsheba back in here!" ordered David.

When she returned, David said to her, "As the Lord lives—the Lord who has rescued me from all my troubles—I'll keep the promise I made in his name! Solomon will become king after me. I'll announce it right now!"

"May my lord King David live forever!" said Bathsheba, bowing low.

"Send for Zadok and Benaiah!" ordered David.

When Zadok the priest and Benaiah the captain of the guard arrived, David said to them, "Take the palace guard and go down to Gihon spring with Solomon. Let him ride my mule. When you arrive, anoint Solomon as king. Sound the ram's horn trumpet and shout, 'Long live King Solomon!' Then bring him back here and let him sit on my throne!"

"So be it!" said Benaiah. "May the Lord your God make your words come true! May the Lord be with Solomon as he has been with you. And may he make Solomon's reign even greater than David's!"

Then Zadok, Benaiah, Nathan, and the palace guards escorted Solomon outside the city to Gihon spring, in the Kidron Valley near En-rogel. Solomon rode down to the spring on David's mule.

When they reached Gihon, Zadok took a container of holy oil and anointed Solomon as king. The people with them sounded the trumpets and shouted, "Long live the king!" Then Solomon rode back up to the city, with the people of Jerusalem following him and shouting with joy. He went into the palace, where he sat on David's throne.

The servants of the king went in to David and congratulated him and praised his son Solomon.

David answered with a prayer.

As he was lying on his bed, David said, "Praise the Lord God of Israel, who has let me live to see one of my sons sitting on the throne of Israel!"

Down at En-rogel, Adonijah and his friends were just finishing their feast when they heard the sound of the trumpets.

"What's that loud noise?" cried Commander Joab, leaping up.

Then a messenger arrived from the palace. It was Jonathan, the son of Abiathar the priest.

"Come here," said Adonijah. "You're a good man. You must be bringing good news."

"I'm afraid not," answered Jonathan. "Our lord King David has made Solomon king. Zadok and Nathan anointed him just now at Gihon. You heard the trumpets and the shouting as they returned to the city. The people are terribly excited. And now Solomon is sitting on David's throne and David's officials are praising him and David is praising God because Solomon is king!"

When Adonijah and his friends heard Jonathan's report, they trembled with fear. What would happen to them now? They jumped up from their seats and hurried off in all directions.

Adonijah ran to the great altar. He put his hands on the horns at the corners of the altar, the holiest place he could touch. Then he cried out, "Let Solomon promise not to put me to death!"

When Solomon heard where his brother was, he said, "If Adonijah will be my loyal subject, I'll see that no harm comes to him. Not a single hair will fall from his head! But if he acts like a traitor, he will die."

Then Solomon sent for Adonijah, who came and bowed down before him. Solomon told him to go home in peace.

Solomon in Power

1 Kings 2

DAVID and Solomon ruled together for a short time. Then one day David called Solomon to his bedside to give him some last words of advice.

"Everyone must die," said the old king. "Now it's my turn. When I'm gone, I want you to be kind to the people who helped me and to punish the people who hurt me.

"Be strong and brave, Solomon. If you follow the Lord's teachings, you'll succeed in everything you do. If you obey his commandments, he will keep the promise he made to me, and one of our family will always rule over Israel."

2

David died and was buried in Jerusalem. He had been king of Judah for seven years and of Judah and Israel for thirty-three years, a total of forty years.

Soon after David's death, Adonijah went to see Bathsheba, the mother of King Solomon. In those days the queen mother was more important than the queen, because the king had so many wives.

"I want to speak to you about something," he said.

"What is it?"

"I'm the oldest son, so I should have become king. You know it. Everyone knows it. Well, it didn't work out. But now you can help me. Please do me a favor."

"Speak!" said Bathsheba.

Adonijah continued, "Please ask the king to do

something for me. I know he'll listen to you. Ask him to let me have Abishag, David's widow. I want to marry her."

"Very well, I'll speak to the king," promised Bathsheba, and she went to see Solomon.

When she arrived, Solomon stood up and bowed to her, and then he gave her a seat next to his throne.

"I have something to ask you," she said. "Please don't refuse me."

"Go ahead, Mother. You know I'll do whatever you ask."

"Please help Adonijah. Let him have Abishag for his wife."

"What?" cried Solomon. "Don't you realize what that means? Adonijah has already tried to make himself king. If I let him marry one of David's widows, he'll try again. His position will be even stronger, and this time he might succeed! Give him Abishag? I might as well give him my throne!"

Solomon was becoming furious. "How dare Adonijah challenge me! The Lord himself has set me on David's throne. May God strike me dead if I don't punish Adonijah for this!"

Then Solomon ordered Captain Benaiah to go and kill Adonijah. As soon as Adonijah was dead, Solomon punished the men who had been supporting him.

He sent for Abiathar the high priest. "You must leave Jerusalem," he said. "Go to your family's land in Anathoth and live there the rest of your life. You deserve to die for helping Adonijah, but I won't kill you, for you stayed with my father through all his troubles."

After Abiathar left, Solomon appointed Zadok the new high priest. For the next eight hundred years the high priests of Israel were members of the family of Zadok. Many years before the time of Solomon, a prophet had told Abiathar's ancestor Eli that disaster would strike his family, that Abiathar would be their last high priest. Now this prophecy was coming true.

Solomon ordered Benaiah to kill Joab, and he made Benaiah commander of the army in Joab's place.

Solomon took care of all the people who had helped David when he was in trouble, and he punished the people who had worked against him.

At last Solomon was in complete control, with no one to challenge his power.

3

The Wisdom of Solomon

1 Kings 3, 5; 2 Chronicles 1

Solomon was very young when he became king—practically a teenager. Yet he was absolute ruler of the united kingdom of Israel and Judah. He also controlled an empire of foreign nations, with territory from the Egyptian border to the Euphrates River, from the Great Western Sea to the eastern desert. He ruled over Arameans in the north, Moabites and Ammonites in the east, Edomites in the south, and Philistines in the west.

One day early in his reign, Solomon went with

21

some of his officials to Gibeon, a town north of Jerusalem. There they worshiped the Lord, and Solomon offered an enormous sacrifice on the great altar.

That night at Gibeon the Lord appeared to Solomon and said, "Ask me what you want me to give you."

Solomon answered, "You have faithfully loved my father, and now you have made me king. O Lord, I'm so young! I don't know how to rule over this great people of yours. Give me wisdom and understanding to govern your people."

"You have made a good choice," said the Lord. "Instead of asking for riches or glory or long life, you have asked for wisdom to rule the people. I'll give you what you have asked for. I'll give you wisdom and understanding greater than anyone has ever had, and greater than anyone ever will have. I'll also give you what you haven't asked for. I'll give you more wealth and honor than any other king. If you follow my teachings and obey my commandments, I'll give you a long life, too!"

Then Solomon woke up. It was a dream.

Back in Jerusalem a few days later, Solomon's dream began to come true. Two women came to ask him to decide a case between them.

"My lord king," said the first woman, "this woman and I live in the same house. I gave birth to a son, and two days later she had a son, too. No one was with us. One night this woman rolled over and smothered her baby in her sleep, and he died. While

I was sleeping, she got up and took my baby from my side and carried him to her bed. Then she put her dead child next to me. When I woke up the next morning, I looked at the baby beside me and I knew he wasn't mine."

"No!" cried the second woman. "That's not true! My son is alive and your son is dead."

"You're lying!" said the first woman. "My child is alive and yours is dead."

As the two women quarreled with each other, the young king turned to a servant and said, "Bring me a sword."

The servant brought the sword, and Solomon ordered, "Take the sword and cut the live baby in two. Give half to each woman."

"My lord king!" cried the first woman. "Don't let them kill the baby. Give it to her!"

"No!" said the second woman. "Neither of us will have it. Go on, cut him up!"

"Stop!" ordered Solomon. "Don't kill the baby. His mother's heart is full of love for him. Give the child to the first woman, for he is hers."

Everyone in Israel heard the story of the two women and the baby, and they realized that Solomon's wisdom came from God.

Building the Temple

1 Kings 5—7; 2 Chronicles 2—4

WHEN David was king, he wanted to build a
house for the Lord—a great place of worship in
Jerusalem. But the Lord told David that Solomon
would be the one to build his house. He promised
David a different kind of house—a royal family of
David's descendants to rule over Israel forever.

Before he died, David gave Solomon the plans for
God's house. It would be a magnificent temple of
white limestone and precious cedar wood, bigger
and more beautiful than any other place of worship.

David and Solomon and the people of Israel knew

that no house on earth could contain almighty God. But in a mysterious way God would be especially with his people in the temple.

Soon after Solomon became king, some messengers arrived in Jerusalem from the Phoenician city of Tyre, on the seacoast north of Israel. King Hiram of Tyre had been friendly with David, and he wanted to be friendly with Solomon, too.

Solomon received Hiram's greeting, and he sent back this message: "I need your help. I'm building a great temple for the Lord, and I need some of the rare and valuable cedar wood which grows in the mountains of Lebanon. Please ask your lumbermen to cut down the trees, for none of my people can do that so well. I'll send workers to help them, and I'll pay your people whatever you ask.

"Send me a master craftsman, too—someone who can work with gold, silver, bronze, and cloth, someone who can teach my people his skills.

"In exchange for all your help, I'll send you supplies of wheat, barley, wine, and olive oil."

Hiram was pleased with Solomon's offer. "Praise the Lord God of Israel!" he said. "The Lord has given David a wise son to rule over his people!"

Hiram ordered his lumbermen to cut down cedars of Lebanon, and Solomon sent workers to help them. They trimmed the logs and dragged them down to the seacoast. Then they tied the logs into rafts and floated them behind ships all the way to the port of Joppa. At Joppa they untied the rafts and loaded the logs into oxcarts to carry them to

Jerusalem. In the rocky hills of Israel other workers dug out huge blocks of limestone.

The cedar logs were made into smooth panels, and the limestone blocks were carefully polished before they were taken up to Mount Moriah, the site of the temple. For this was a holy place, chosen by the Lord himself, and no sound of hammer or chisel was allowed.

In the fourth year of Solomon's reign, the preparations were complete, and the foundation of the temple was laid.

King Hiram's master craftsman, Huramabi, designed the decorations and the furniture for the temple. He taught the Israelites how to carve wood, engrave gold and silver, and mold bronze in huge casts.

They wove cloth, dyed it brilliant shades of red, blue, and purple, and embroidered it with beautiful pictures of flowers, trees, and animals.

Seven years after the foundation was laid, the temple was finished. The great white stone temple of God stood at last on the top of the highest hill in Jerusalem, facing east, toward the rising sun.

In front of the temple building was a large open place called the courtyard. A thick wall of white limestone and cedar wood surrounded the temple and the courtyard.

This open courtyard was divided into two parts—an outer court where the people worshiped, and an inner court where the priests

sacrificed the offerings. In the priests' court stood a great bronze altar and great bronze containers of water for washing the offerings.

In front of the temple building stood two enormous bronze pillars, one on each side of the entrance. Alongside the other three sides of the temple were rooms for storage of equipment and treasure.

The inside of the temple was small, for the worship services were held outside, in the courtyard. The inside of the temple was divided into three rooms, all covered with cedar panels and overlaid with pure gold. Even the floor of the temple was gold. The gold was engraved with lovely designs of palm trees and patterns of chains.

The first room was the entrance hall, or porch. Behind a golden door was the main room, called the holy place. In the holy place were ten golden tables, ten golden lampstands, and a golden altar for burning incense.

A double door covered with golden chains separated the holy place from the secret inner room, the holy of holies. In front of the door hung an embroidered curtain called the veil.

The holy of holies was smaller than the other rooms. It contained just one piece of furniture, the ark of the covenant. The ark was a golden box, containing the two stone tablets of the law that the Lord had given to Moses.

In front of the ark stood two large golden

figures called cherubs. They were fierce beasts with great, outstretched wings. They resembled the wild animals that guarded the thrones of earthly kings.

The ark was the footstool of the invisible throne of Israel's invisible king, the Lord God himself. And when the temple was completed, the Lord came to his house.

Solomon's Prayer and God's Warning

1 Kings 8—9; 2 Chronicles 5—7

SOLOMON invited all the people of Israel to come to Jerusalem for a great service to dedicate the temple, to set it apart for the worship of the Lord.

The priests brought the ark into the holy of holies and set it down behind the golden cherubs. As they were leaving, the glory of the Lord suddenly appeared as a pillar of cloud, filling the temple with a bright, unearthly light. This was the sign that the Lord had come to make his home among his people.

When Solomon saw the glory of the Lord, he said,

O Lord, who put the sun in the sky,
you have chosen to hide in a thick cloud.

Here we have built a great house for you,
a place for you to be with your people forever!

Then Solomon turned and faced the people and blessed them, saying, "Thanks be to the Lord God of Israel! He has kept the promise he made to my father, David!"

Solomon climbed up onto a platform in the

middle of the courtyard. He knelt down, raised his hands toward heaven, and prayed.

"O Lord God of Israel," he prayed. "There is no one like you in heaven above or on earth below! You keep your promises, and you show mercy to your people.

"Now, Lord God, hear my prayer. Watch over this house night and day. Protect this temple. Listen to the prayers of your people. You, and you only, O God, know all our secret thoughts. Teach us to do what is right. Listen to us when we pray to you for help. Listen to us when we confess our sins. Be merciful, Lord, and forgive us.

"Bless your priests and help them in their work. For the sake of your love for David, don't reject your anointed kings. Let one of David's family sit on the throne of Israel forever."

Then Solomon went to the front of the altar, and he cried out in a loud voice, "Thanks be to God, who helps his people! May he always be with us. And may we always be faithful to him, so all the people on earth will know that the Lord and only the Lord is God."

That day Solomon and the people offered many sacrifices to the Lord on the great bronze altar. The Lord accepted their sacrifices, and as a sign, he sent fire down from the sky to burn up the offerings.

When the people saw the lightning strike the altar, they bowed down and prayed. The musicians praised the Lord with their cymbals, harps, and lyres. They sang,

Praise to the Lord,
   for he is good,
And his mercy is everlasting!

The people of Israel celebrated at the temple for seven days. They sang and shouted and clapped their hands, praising the Lord their God with all their might.

On the eighth day Solomon sent the people home, rejoicing in the goodness of their God.

One night soon after this, the Lord appeared to Solomon in another dream. He said, "I have heard your prayers, and I'll answer the prayers of the people. This temple will be my house, and I'll watch over it forever. If you follow my teachings and obey my commandments, one of your family will rule over Israel forever."

Then the Lord gave Solomon a warning. "If you or your family disobey me," he said, "if you refuse to follow my teachings, if you worship other gods— then I will leave this temple. I'll let your enemies come and destroy it. The temple will fall into ruins, and people everywhere will laugh and make fun of Israel.

"Those who pass by the ruins of the temple will be so shocked, they'll ask why this terrible thing happened. 'Why did the Lord do this to this land and this temple?' they will say. And someone will answer, 'Because the people left the Lord their God.'

"Let this be a warning to you and all the people of Israel."

6

Solomon and the Queen of Sheba

1 Kings 4—5, 7, 9—10; 2 Chronicles 1, 8—9

AFTER he built the temple for the Lord, Solomon built a palace for himself. It took seven years to build the temple and thirteen years to build the palace.

Solomon's palace stood on a hill just below the temple. It was made of white limestone and cedar wood, like the temple. The main building of the palace had so many cedar pillars, it was called "The Hall of the Forest of Lebanon."

Solomon had a magnificent throne decorated with precious carved ivory and a footstool made of

gold. Twelve figures of lions stood on the six steps leading up to his throne, one on each side of each step. Another pair of lions stood beside the armrests of the throne.

Solomon built fortresses all over the land, and he kept thousands of horses and chariots in the fortresses and in Jerusalem. He replaced the old system of twelve tribes with a strong central government. The people sent food to Solomon's household and paid taxes of grain and other crops, which were kept in government storehouses.

Many years earlier the prophet Samuel had warned the people what kings would do to them.

Now his words were beginning to come true. All of Solomon's building projects were carried out by forced labor and paid for with high taxes. Solomon put an official named Adoram in charge of the labor, forcing the people of Israel to work on his building projects.

Solomon was as rich as he was powerful. He controlled the important overland caravan routes through Israel, gaining wealth from land trade. And King Hiram of Tyre helped Solomon become a sea trader.

The Phoenicians were the greatest sailors of the ancient world. Hiram invited Solomon to send his fleet to sail with the Phoenicians to the western lands of the Great Sea. He also sent ships and sailors to go with Solomon's men to India, Arabia, and the east coast of Africa. They came back with rare wood, jewels, ivory, ebony, and gold. They also brought strange animals for the royal zoo—apes and baboons.

Solomon built a seaport at Ezion-geber on the shore of the Red Sea. There he had shipyards and copper and bronze works.

Solomon was so wealthy, people in other countries heard about him. They heard that gold and silver were as common as pebbles in the streets of Jerusalem. They heard that Solomon had so much gold, all the furniture in his palace was made of gold, the palace guards carried golden shields, and Solomon himself drank from cups made of pure gold.

Some foreign kings sent valuable gifts to honor King Solomon. Others made visits to meet him.

One day a rich queen arrived in Jerusalem with many servants and camels. She had traveled over a thousand miles across the great eastern desert, all the way from her kingdom on the shore of South Arabia, a land rich from the trade of rare spices and perfumes. She was the queen of Sheba.

The queen of Sheba had heard so much about Solomon's wisdom, she tested him with riddles. She asked him questions about everything she could think of.

Solomon had answers to all her questions. He could talk about any subject. He recited some of his wise sayings for her, and he sang some of the songs he had composed.

Then he invited the queen of Sheba to eat at his table, and he showed her the buildings he had made. He took her to see the great houses of his nobles and the magnificent temple of the Lord. He showed her the golden rooms of the temple and the ivory throne in the palace.

It all took her breath away.

"I've heard many things about you in my own country," she said. "I didn't believe them until I saw for myself. But everything I heard is true—and I only heard half of it. You're even richer and wiser than they say. How happy are your servants, who hear your wisdom every day. How happy are your wives. Praise to the Lord your God, who loves Israel so much—he has made you king!"

Then the queen of Sheba gave Solomon the gifts she had brought: tons of gold, a large number of jewels, and great quantities of precious spices and perfumes.

Solomon gave her everything she wanted, and then the queen of Sheba returned to her own country.

7

Solomon's Foolishness

1 Kings 3, 5, 11; 2 Chronicles 9

GOD kept his promises. He blessed Solomon and gave him wisdom, wealth, and glory greater than any other king. Solomon was wiser than the famous wise men of the East. His wisdom was greater than all the wisdom of Egypt. He was the wisest man and the richest king in the world.

At the beginning of his reign Solomon married the daughter of the king of Egypt, and the king of Egypt gave him the city of Gezer as a wedding present. Throughout his life Solomon married hundreds of foreign women, as well as many Israelites. Even though the Lord had warned his people not to marry heathen women, Solomon married Hittites, Moabites, Ammonites, Arameans, Edomites, and Phoenicians, and he loved them all.

Most of these marriages were made to create alliances with other nations. These alliances were good for trade and the safety of the kingdom. Solomon wanted to please his foreign wives, so he built altars where they could burn incense and offer sacrifices to their gods.

At the end of the long life which the Lord had given to him, Solomon began to love his wives more than the Lord. He began to go with them to their altars and to worship their gods. He worshiped Asherah, the goddess of the Phoenicians, Molech, the god of the Ammonites, and Chemosh, the god of the Moabites.

The Lord was so angry, he said to Solomon, "You've been unfaithful to me! You haven't followed my teachings. You haven't obeyed my commandments. For this reason, I'm going to tear the kingdom away from you and give it to one of your servants. But for the sake of your father, David, I won't do this in your lifetime; and I won't take the whole kingdom away. I'll let your son become king after you, and I'll leave him with one tribe to rule over."

One day Solomon went out to inspect some repair work on the walls of Jerusalem. He noticed a young nobleman from the tribe of Ephraim, a man named Jeroboam. He was so impressed with Jeroboam, he

put him in charge of the workers in Ephraim.

Some time later Jeroboam happened to be walking on the road outside Jerusalem. A prophet named Ahijah came up to him in the open country and took off the new cloak he was wearing.

Ahijah tore the cloak into twelve pieces and then he said, "Take ten pieces for yourself, Jeroboam. The Lord God of Israel has said he will tear the kingdom away from Solomon and give it to you. He'll let Solomon's son become king, and he'll give him one tribe to rule over. If you obey the Lord and follow his teachings, he'll be with you. He'll build a lasting house for you and your family, as he has done for David."

When King Solomon found out about this, he tried to have Jeroboam killed. But Jeroboam escaped to Egypt, and he stayed there until Solomon died.

Before the end of Solomon's reign, the Lord raised up enemies against him, who weakened his empire. Hadad, an Edomite prince, rebelled and made Edom an independent kingdom. Rezon, an Aramean army officer, captured the city of Damascus and made himself king, rebelling against the rule of Solomon.

After ruling over Israel for forty years, Solomon died. In spite of all his wisdom, he had foolishly turned away from the Lord, and his kingdom was about to fall apart.

The Kingdom Is Divided

8

The Kingdom Is Torn Away

1 Kings 12; 2 Chronicles 10—11

SOLOMON'S son Rehoboam was crowned king in Jerusalem by the people of the tribe of Judah. Then the people of the northern tribes of Israel invited Rehoboam to meet with them at Shechem, a town in the central hill country north of Jerusalem.

When Rehoboam arrived at Shechem, the leaders of the ten tribes said to him, "Before we accept you as our king, you must make an agreement with us. Your father, King Solomon, gave us heavy burdens to bear. He made us pay high taxes and he forced us to work on his building projects. If you lighten our burdens, we'll be your loyal subjects."

Rehoboam was young and inexperienced. He didn't know what to do. "Give me three days," he said. "I'll have an answer for you then."

Rehoboam went to see the old men who had been Solomon's advisers. "What answer should I give these people?" he asked them.

The old men answered, "If you want to be a good king, treat the people fairly. Lighten their burdens, and they'll be your loyal subjects."

Then Rehoboam went to the young noblemen who had grown up with him. "What answer should I give these people?" he asked them.

The young men told Rehoboam to say to the people,

My little finger is thicker than my father's waist!

My father made your burdens heavy;
I'll make them even heavier.

He beat you with lashes;
I'll sting you with bullwhips!

On the third day the leaders of the ten northern tribes returned to hear Rehoboam's answer. He said,

My little finger is thicker than my father's waist!

My father made your burdens heavy;
I'll make them even heavier.

He beat you with lashes;
I'll sting you with bullwhips!

When the leaders of Israel heard this answer,
they shouted,

What do we care about David's house?
His family means nothing to us!

Let's go home, men of Israel.
Let David's family take care of their own tribe!

Then the men of Israel attacked Adoram, the official in charge of the forced labor, and they stoned
him to death. Rehoboam quickly got into his chariot
and raced back to Jerusalem.
The leaders of the ten northern tribes heard that

Jeroboam had returned from Egypt. They invited him to meet with them, and they crowned him as their king.

Meanwhile, Rehoboam reached Jerusalem and gathered together his best warriors. He prepared to attack the northern tribes.

Then the word of the Lord came to a prophet named Shemaiah. He took this message to King Rehoboam: "The Lord says not to fight your brothers of the ten northern tribes. Send the soldiers home, for what has happened is the will of God."

Rehoboam obeyed the word of the Lord and sent his soldiers home.

That is how Solomon's kingdom was torn away from Solomon's son. Instead of the strong united kingdom of David and Solomon, now there were two weak kingdoms. Jeroboam ruled over ten tribes in the north, and Rehoboam ruled over one tribe in the south.

Jeroboam's kingdom was known as the kingdom of Israel, or Ephraim, after the largest and most important tribe. Sometimes it was called Samaria, for one of its capital cities.

Rehoboam's kingdom was called the kingdom of Judah. The kingdom of Judah included part of the small tribe of Benjamin as well as David's tribe of Judah.

All of God's people together were known as Israel, or the twelve tribes of Israel.

The kingdom of Israel had three times as much territory as the kingdom of Judah. It extended north to the city of Dan and south to the city of Bethel. It also included Gilead, the territory on the eastern side of the Jordan River.

Judah's land was smaller and poorer than Israel's. But Judah contained the palace of Solomon and the temple of the Lord. And the kings of Judah were descendants of David, whom God had promised to be rulers of his people forever.

9

The Sin of Jeroboam

1 Kings 12—14

JEROBOAM was worried. Every year the people of Israel went to the temple in Jerusalem for the great fall festival. He said to himself, "If they keep on going to the temple, they'll start supporting the family of David. They'll become Rehoboam's loyal subjects, and then what will happen to me? They'll kill me. I must stop them!"

Jeroboam didn't trust God's promises. Instead, he tried to strengthen his position all by himself. He set up places of worship on hilltops all over Israel and in the cities of Dan and Bethel. He made images of calves for the people to worship and invited them to come to his fall festival at Bethel.

"People of Israel!" cried Jeroboam. "See these golden calves. Here are your gods who brought you out of Egypt!"

The golden calves looked just like the idols of Baal, the god of the Canaanites. Jeroboam set one calf up in the temple at Dan and the other at the temple at Bethel. He encouraged the people to worship the golden calves, which was a great sin against the Lord.

Priests who were loyal to the Lord refused to serve Jeroboam's idols. They left Israel and moved to Judah, and many other people who loved the Lord went with them.

Jeroboam replaced the priests of the Lord with priests of his own. He ignored the Lord's rule that all priests should belong to the family of Aaron, the brother of Moses.

Jeroboam did these things because he loved his own power more than he loved the Lord. This sin of Jeroboam brought the destruction of his family and his kingdom.

One day while Jeroboam was at the great altar at Bethel, a prophet came from Judah with a message. The prophet arrived just as Jeroboam was standing on the steps in front of the altar, about to offer a sacrifice to the golden calf.

"O altar!" cried the prophet. "The Lord says that one day a king of Judah named Josiah will come here and destroy this altar and the priests who serve here. This is the sign that my words are true: the altar will fall apart and its ashes will scatter, for the Lord refuses to accept your worthless sacrifices."

When Jeroboam heard this prophecy, he stretched out his arm and pointed at the prophet. "Seize that man!" he ordered.

At that very moment Jeroboam's hand became paralyzed, and he couldn't move it. And the altar burst apart and its ashes scattered to the ground.

"Please!" cried Jeroboam. "I beg you, ask the Lord to heal my arm."

The prophet prayed to the Lord, and Jeroboam's arm was healed.

But even after this warning, Jeroboam didn't change his evil ways. He wasn't sorry, and he didn't turn back to the Lord. Then the Lord sent him an even more terrible message.

Jeroboam's oldest son became ill. Jeroboam said to his wife, "Please go to Shiloh, to the house of Abijah, the prophet who tore his cloak and said that I would become king. Go in disguise, and take him a present of cakes and honey. He'll tell you what will happen to our child."

Jeroboam's wife did as he said. She left their home in Tirzah and traveled to Ahijah's house in Shiloh. She went in disguise, taking presents for the prophet.

The Lord told Ahijah that Jeroboam's wife was coming, so even though he was old and nearly blind, he recognized her when she arrived.

"Come in, wife of Jeroboam!" he called. "Why are you in disguise?"

After she came in, Ahijah said, "I have bad news for you. The Lord has given me a message for Jeroboam."

Then Ahijah repeated the Lord's message: "Ever since I raised you up to lead my people," said the Lord, "you have turned away from me. You have disobeyed me and you have led my people into worshiping idols. Because of this, I won't build a

lasting house for you and your family. Instead, I'll wipe out all the men of your family and sweep them away like garbage!"

Then Ahijah said to Jeroboam's wife, "Go home. As soon as you arrive, your son will die. In the future the Lord will raise up a new king, who will destroy Jeroboam's family. The Lord will bring troubles to Israel. He'll strike Israel until it trembles like a reed in the water!"

Jeroboam's wife went home. As soon as she entered the house, the child died.

A few years later, Jeroboam died and his son Nadab became king of Israel.

10

The Lord Brings Victory to Judah

1 Kings 14—15; 2 Chronicles 11—16

WHILE Jeroboam, king of Israel, was worshiping idols, Rehoboam, king of Judah, was worshiping the Lord.

The Lord gave Rehoboam peace for the first few years of his reign, and during this time Rehoboam built up the defenses of his kingdom. He strengthened the fortresses which Solomon had built, and he built fifteen new fortresses in towns around Jerusalem. He stationed soldiers and supplies in the fortresses, ready to defeat any enemy.

But then Rehoboam and his people began to worship idols. They put up stone pillars and images of the goddess Asherah on every hill and under every tree. They copied the shameful behavior of the Canaanites, and they ignored the teachings of the Lord their God.

The Lord sent Shishak, king of Egypt, to punish Rehoboam and the people of Judah. The Egyptian army invaded Judah with a great number of horses and chariots. Rehoboam's strong fortresses were helpless against them.

While Shishak and his men prepared to attack Jerusalem, Rehoboam and his commanders hid inside the city. They were terrified of the Egyptians.

Then the Lord sent a prophet named Shemaiah to Rehoboam. Shemaiah said, "You have turned away from the Lord, so he is turning you over to Shishak!"

Rehoboam and his commanders confessed their sins, and the Lord heard their prayers.

A few days later Shemaiah returned with another message from the Lord. He said, "Because you have humbled yourselves and confessed your sins, the Lord won't let Shishak destroy Jerusalem."

Shishak came into the city and took gold from the temple and the palace, but he didn't destroy Jerusalem.

When Rehoboam died, his son Abijam became king of Judah. Abijam reigned for three years. During that time the kingdom of Judah was at war with the kingdom of Israel. Abijam's army was pitifully small, only half the size of Jeroboam's army. But

Abijam trusted the Lord, and the Lord gave him victory over Jeroboam.

After Abijam died, his son Asa was king. Asa ruled for more than forty years. His early reign was a time of peace, and he rebuilt the fortress cities with stronger, solid stone walls and towers and gates with locks.

Then one year an Ethiopian named Zerah attacked with a huge army. Asa turned to the Lord and prayed, "O Lord, you can help a small, weak army as easily as you can help a great, powerful one. Help us now, O Lord our God, for we're depending on you!"

The Lord answered Asa's prayer. He helped

Judah's small, weak army by sending panic to the Ethiopians, causing them to run away.

Soon after this victory, a prophet named Azariah came to see Asa. He said, "The Lord will be with you as long as you and your people obey his commandments. But if you turn away from the Lord, he'll turn away from you. Be strong and brave, for your good works will be rewarded."

Asa felt encouraged by Azariah's message. He told the people of Judah to tear down the high places and to get rid of their idols. He even destroyed an idol that belonged to his mother, Queen Maacah, and he took away her privileges as Queen Mother.

Asa called the people of Judah to come to the temple for a great worship service. They agreed to serve the Lord with all their hearts and minds, and the Lord blessed them.

Toward the end of Asa's reign, Judah was once more at war with Israel. This time Asa took gold and silver from the palace and the temple and sent it to Ben-Hadad, king of Damascus. Ben-Hadad agreed to help Asa by sending his army to attack the Israelites. The Israelites stopped attacking Judah and went to fight the Arameans.

Asa was pleased with himself for saving his kingdom by buying help from Ben-Hadad. He was annoyed when a prophet named Hanani came to him with a warning.

Hanani said, "You trusted the Lord when the Ethiopians attacked. The Lord saved you then. Why didn't you keep on trusting the Lord—he would have given you a great victory over Israel!"

Asa was so angry, he put Hanani in prison. At the same time, he began to treat his people cruelly.

Asa became ill, but he didn't pray to the Lord. Instead, he sent for magicians to cure him. Then Asa died, and his son Jehoshaphat became king of Judah.

11

The Lord Brings Trouble to Israel

1 Kings 15—16

DURING the long reign of King Asa of Judah, many different kings reigned in Israel. The Lord brought troubles to Israel and struck the kingdom until it trembled like a reed in water. Four kings were assassinated and their families were wiped out.

Jeroboam's son Nadab ruled for just two years. He worshiped idols, as his father did.

One day an army officer named Baasha plotted against Nadab and killed him. Baasha made himself king, and then he destroyed Jeroboam's whole family, just as Ahijah the prophet had said.

Baasha ruled for twenty-four years. During this time the Arameans of Damascus were so strong they took over Israel's territory in Gilead.

Baasha was an idol-worshiper like Jeroboam and Nadab, so the Lord sent a prophet named Jehu to warn him. Jehu said, "The Lord raised you up from the ground and made you ruler over his people. But you have followed the example of Jeroboam, and you have led his people into sin. Because of this, the Lord is going to destroy you and your family, as he destroyed the family of Jeroboam."

When Baasha died, his son Elah became king of Israel. Baasha's son Elah was like Jeroboam's son Nadab. He ruled for only two years and then was assassinated by one of his officers.

A chariot captain named Zimri plotted against Elah and killed him while he was getting drunk in the house of one of his officials. Then Zimri made himself king. He destroyed Baasha's whole family, just as Jehu the prophet had said.

But Zimri wasn't able to rule the kingdom, for most of the soldiers refused to support him. They followed a commander named Omri, marching with him to attack Zimri at Tirzah. Zimri hid inside the fortress of the palace, set it on fire, and died in the flames. His reign was the shortest of all—just seven days.

About half the people in the kingdom supported Omri and the rest wanted an officer named Tibni to be king. For five years there was civil war between

the followers of Omri and the followers of Tibni. Finally, Omri defeated Tibni, united the kingdom, and ruled as king of Israel.

Omri was a rich and powerful ruler. He moved the capital city from Tirzah to a place farther west in the high hills of central Israel. He built a new city on a high hill and named it Samaria. The city was so strong, it was able to keep out enemies for hundreds of years.

During Omri's reign Israel was at war with the Moabites and the Arameans. The Arameans were the most dangerous enemy. Omri made an alliance with the Phoenicians to help him against the Arameans. He arranged for his son Ahab to marry Jezebel, the daughter of Ethbaal, king of Tyre. Ethbaal was a priest of the goddess Asherah. He had become king the same way as Zimri and Omri—by overthrowing the reigning king.

Omri and Ethbaal also made a trading agreement.

After Omri's death, his son Ahab became king of Israel. Ahab sometimes tried to do the right thing, but most of the time he was under the influence of his evil wife, Queen Jezebel. He did more than all the kings who ruled before him to make the Lord angry with Israel.

Stories About Elijah

12

God Sends Elijah

1 Kings 17

AHAB and Jezebel led the people of Israel into more sin than ever. In the capital city of Samaria, Ahab built a great temple for Baal, the Canaanite god of thunder and rain. He also built an altar and an image of Asherah, the Canaanite goddess of fertility. Jezebel hated the Lord so much, she killed all of his prophets that she could find.

The Lord sent a man named Elijah to fight against Ahab and Jezebel and the idol worshipers of Israel. Elijah was from Gilead, the eastern part of the kingdom. God gave him power to teach the people and to do miracles. His name, Elijah, meant "My God is the Lord."

Elijah lived all alone in the wilderness. From time to time he suddenly appeared in the cities, looking out of place in his unusual cloak, a mantle made of animal skin, and his leather loincloth.

One day Elijah came to King Ahab and said, "As surely as the Lord lives, it won't rain in this land for three years!"

No rain meant no water for plants, animals, or people. The Lord was going to hold back the rain to punish Israel for worshiping Baal, the god of rain.

After Elijah made this announcement to Ahab, the Lord said to him, "Go away from here and hide in the Cherith Valley. There you can drink water from a stream, and I'll send ravens to feed you."

Elijah obeyed the Lord's command. He went out to the Valley of Cherith, east of the Jordan River. He drank water from the stream, and every morning big black ravens brought him bread. Every evening the same birds brought him meat.

No rain fell, and the stream began to dry up. Soon it was completely empty, and Elijah had nothing to drink.

"Get up," the Lord said to him. "Go to the town of Zarephath, near Sidon. I've commanded a widow there to feed you."

Elijah went north to the land of the Phoenicians, as the Lord commanded. At the gate of Zarephath, he saw a woman dressed in widow's clothes. She was picking up dry sticks.

"Please bring me a small cup of water," Elijah said to her. As she went to fetch it, he called after her, "Please bring me a little piece of bread, too."

"As the Lord lives," said the woman, "I have no bread. I have only a little bit of flour in a jar and a little bit of oil in a jug. I came out here to gather a few sticks to burn, so I can cook the flour and oil for myself and my son. When it's gone, we'll starve to death."

"Don't be afraid," said Elijah. "Go home and cook for yourself. But first make a little loaf of bread for me. For the Lord has said,

'The flour jar won't be empty,
   and the oil jar won't run out
Until the Lord sends rain
   and ends this awful drought.' "

The woman went and did as Elijah told her. She made him a little loaf of bread, and another one for herself and her son. But the flour jar wasn't empty, and the oil jar didn't run out, just as Elijah had said to her.

The Phoenician widow invited Elijah to stay in her house as a guest. They all had enough to eat that day and every day, just using the flour and oil in the jars.

One day the widow's son became seriously ill. He grew worse and worse until he stopped breathing.

"O man of God!" cried the woman. "Why has this terrible thing happpened to me?"

"Give me your son," said Elijah. He took the boy from her arms and carried him upstairs and laid him down on his own bed.

"O Lord, my God," cried Elijah, "Why have you done this? This woman has helped me, and now you have brought her trouble and sorrow."

Elijah stretched himself out on the child's body three times and prayed, "O Lord, my God, may the breath of life return to this little boy."

The Lord heard Elijah's prayer, and the child began to breathe again.

Elijah carried the boy down to his mother. "Look!" he said to her. "Your son is alive!"

She looked at him and said, "Now I know that you're a man of God. What you say is the word of the Lord, and it is the truth."

13

The Contest Between Elijah and the Prophets of Baal

1 Kings 18

No rain fell in Israel for three years. The streams and rivers dried up, the grass died, and the plants couldn't grow. There was hardly any food or water for the animals and people. The famine was the worst in Ahab's capital of Samaria.

In the third year of the drought, the Lord said to Elijah, "Go to Ahab, for I'm about to send rain to end this drought."

Elijah started to go to Ahab's palace in Samaria. On the way he met Obadiah, a servant of the king who worshiped the Lord. When Jezebel was slaughtering the prophets of the Lord, Obadiah hid a hundred of them and took care of them. Now he was out looking for water for the king's horses.

When Obadiah saw Elijah, he bowed down to the ground and said, "So here you are, my lord Elijah!"

"Yes," answered Elijah. "Go tell your master that I'm here."

"Don't ask me to do that," said Obadiah. "It would be the end of me! The king has been looking for you everywhere. If I tell him I have found you and then you disappear, he'll kill me!"

"As the Lord lives," promised Elijah, "I won't disappear. I'll go see the king this very day!"

Obadiah went and told Ahab that he had found Elijah. Ahab immediately went out to meet him.

When he saw Elijah, Ahab said, "So here you are, you troublemaker in Israel."

"I'm not the troublemaker," answered Elijah. "It's you and your family who are making trouble for Israel. This drought came because you're worshiping the images of Baal."

Then Elijah said to Ahab, "The drought will soon end. Tell the people to come to Mount Carmel. You come, too, and bring the prophets of Baal with you. Bring all four hundred and fifty of them, the ones your wife, Jezebel, supports. We'll have a contest to find out who's really God in Israel!"

Ahab told the people and the prophets of Baal to go to Mount Carmel, north of Samaria on the shore of the Great Sea. The people prepared by fasting. They didn't eat anything all day, hoping to please God, so he would send the rain.

The next morning Elijah met them at the foot of the mountain. He stood in front of the people and said, "How much longer are you going to hop back and forth on one foot and then the other, not choosing either side? Make up your minds! If the Lord is God, follow him. But if Baal is god, follow him!"

The people said nothing.

Then Elijah said, "Of all the prophets of the Lord, I'm the only one left. And there are four hundred and fifty prophets of Baal in Israel! Now let's see whose god is truly God. Bring two oxen and let the prophets of Baal make an altar, choose an ox, and prepare it as an offering for their god. Have them put the offering on the altar without setting fire to it. I'll prepare the other ox. Let the prophets of Baal pray to their god, and I'll pray to mine. The god who answers by sending fire to his altar is the true God."

"We agree," said the people.

Then Elijah said to the prophets of Baal, "Since there are so many of you, you go first. Prepare the offering and pray to your god. But don't light the fire."

The prophets of Baal did as Elijah said. They made an altar, prepared the offering, and put it on the wood. Then they called on the name of Baal. They prayed to him from morning to noon. They cried out, "O Baal! Great lord of the sky! God of rain, lord of thunder and lightning! Answer us."

But there was no answer, no voice.

The prophets of Baal danced around the altar with hopping steps, first on one foot and then the other. But still no answer came.

In the middle of the day, Elijah began to tease them. "Call louder!" he said. "Surely Baal is a god. Maybe he's too busy to answer you. Maybe he has gone on a journey, or he's sleeping and you must wake him up."

The prophets of Baal shouted louder. They cut themselves with knives until they bled, according to their custom. They ranted and raved all afternoon. But it was no use. No answer came. Their god of thunder and lightning paid no attention. No fire struck Baal's altar.

"Come over here by me," said Elijah to the people.

As they gathered around him, Elijah built an altar for the Lord and dug a trench around it. He arranged wood on the altar and put the offering on the wood.

Then he said, "Fill four pots with water and pour the water over the offering."

They did as he said.

"Do it again," said Elijah.

They poured water over the offering again.

"Do it a third time," he said.

They soaked the offering and the wood and the altar until the water flowed down the sides of the altar and filled up the trench.

Then Elijah went up to the altar and prayed, "O Lord God of Abraham, Isaac, and Jacob. Show these people today that you are God in Israel! Show them that I'm your servant and I've done all these things at your command. Win these people back to yourself, Lord."

At that moment, the Lord sent fire down from the sky. It struck the altar and burned up the offering and the wood. It dried up the water in the trench, too.

"The Lord is God! The Lord is really God!"

cried the people, and they bowed to the ground.

"Seize the prophets of Baal!" shouted Elijah. "Don't let any of them get away."

The people grabbed the four hundred and fifty prophets of Baal, and Elijah ordered all of them put to death, for they had led Israel into sin.

"Now," said Elijah to Ahab, "get up and eat and drink. The rain will soon be here and the drought will be over. I hear the sound of a storm coming."

Ahab and the people left, and Elijah climbed to the top of Mount Carmel with his servant. He bowed down to pray, and then he said to the servant, "Go look out toward the sea."

The servant went and looked, and then he came back. "There's nothing there at all," he reported.

"Go and look seven times," said Elijah.

The servant went and looked again and again. After the seventh time he came back. "I saw a little cloud," he said. "It was as small as a man's hand, rising up from the sea."

"Go!" ordered Elijah. "Tell Ahab to harness his chariot and return home before the rain comes."

The sky grew dark with thick clouds, the wind began to blow, and a heavy rain poured down.

Ahab harnessed his chariot and started for Jezreel, a city near Carmel, where he had another palace.

Then the power of the Lord came over Elijah, and he tucked up his mantle and ran in front of Ahab all the way from Mount Carmel to Jezreel.

14

Elijah Hears a Quiet Voice

1 Kings 19

WHEN Ahab arrived at his palace, he told Jezebel what had happened at Mount Carmel. Jezebel was so angry, she sent a messenger to Elijah, saying, "May the gods punish me if you're not as dead as my prophets by this time tomorrow!"

Elijah was frightened, and he took his servant and ran away. He traveled south, through the kingdom of Israel and into Judah. When he reached Beersheba, in southern Judah, he left the servant. He continued on alone into the wilderness. Finally, he stopped walking and sat down in the shade of a small tree. He was exhausted.

"It's too much, Lord," cried Elijah. "Take my life! I might as well be dead." Then he lay down and went to sleep.

Suddenly Elijah felt someone touch him. It was an angel, a messenger from the Lord.

"Get up and eat," said the angel.

Elijah looked around. On the ground next to him he found a warm loaf of bread and a jar of water. He ate and drank and lay down again.

The angel touched him once more and said, "Get up and eat, or the journey will be too much for you."

Elijah got up, ate some more bread, and drank some more water. He felt stronger, and he began to walk into the great rocky wilderness of Sinai. After forty days and forty nights, he reached Mount Sinai, the holy mountain of God, where the Lord had revealed himself to Moses.

Elijah found an opening in a large rock beside the mountain. He went into this cave to spend the night.

Then the Lord told Elijah to go out and stand on the mountain. When he did, the Lord himself passed by.

Elijah felt a mighty wind, so strong that it tore the mountain and broke the rocks into pieces. But the Lord was not in the wind.

After the wind came an earthquake, so strong that the whole mountain shook. But the Lord was

not in the earthquake.

After the earthquake came fire, but the Lord was not in the fire.

After the fire came the sound of a gentle breeze, and the Lord was there.

Elijah covered his face with his mantle and went out and stood at the entrance of the cave. He was afraid to look at the Lord God.

"What are you doing here, Elijah?" asked the quiet voice.

Elijah answered, "I've been your faithful follower, Lord. I've called the people to come back to you, but they have smashed your altars and killed your prophets. I'm the only one left, and now they're trying to kill me!"

"Go," said the voice of the Lord. "Return the same way you came. I have three things for you to do. First, find a man named Elisha and call him to be your helper. He will be my prophet after you. Then find Hazael and call him to be king of Damascus. Third, find commander Jehu and anoint him to be king of Israel.

"This is what will happen," said the Lord. "Hazael, king of the Arameans, will kill many of the idol worshipers of Israel. Those who escape from him will be killed by Jehu. And those who escape from Jehu will be killed by Elisha.

"But I will spare seven thousand people in Israel," he promised. "I will save everyone who has not bowed down and worshiped Baal!"

Elijah left the mountain and returned the same way he had come. When he reached the town of Abel Meholah, he saw some young men plowing in a field, with oxen pulling their plows. One of them was the young man, Elisha.

Elijah went up to him and threw his hairy mantle over Elisha's shoulders. As he did, the power of Elijah came over Elisha, and the young man left his plow and ran after Elijah.

"I'll follow you," he said, "but first let me kiss my father and mother good-bye."

"Do as you wish," said Elijah.

Elisha went back, slaughtered the oxen, and ate a farewell meal with his family and friends. Then he said good-bye to them forever. He left everything to follow Elijah.

15

Ahab Steals a Vineyard

1 Kings 20—21

AHAB, king of Israel, was a rich and powerful man. He owned hundreds of horses and camels which he kept in great stables at the city of Megiddo. He had two beautiful palaces, one at Jezreel and one at Samaria, the city his father, Omri, had built. Ahab enlarged the city of Samaria and built some new cities. He decorated his palace in Samaria with expensive ivory carvings.

The Lord gave Ahab victory over the Arameans, and then Ahab made an alliance with

Ben-Hadad, king of the Arameans. Ben-Hadad returned some of the territory in Gilead he had captured earlier.

Yet, with all his wealth, power, and success, Ahab wasn't satisfied. He wanted more.

Next to Ahab's palace in Jezreel was a vineyard which belonged to a man named Naboth. There was nothing special about it, but Ahab wanted it.

"Let me have your vineyard," he said to Naboth. "I want to use the land for a vegetable garden. I'll give you a better one to take its place. Or, if you prefer, I'll pay for it in silver."

"God forbid!" answered Naboth. "This land has been in my family since the Lord brought us into this country. I'll never sell it!"

Ahab could not stand not getting what he wanted. He went home and lay down on his couch, turned his face to the wall, and refused to eat.

When Jezebel saw Ahab sulking, she asked, "Why are you so sad? Why don't you eat?"

"I want Naboth's vineyard," said Ahab, "and he won't sell it to me."

"Well, a fine king you are! Come on, cheer up and eat. I'll get that land for you myself."

One of God's laws for Israel was that land should stay in the same family, so each family could earn its living from the land and no family would become poor. Jezebel understood the law, although she had no respect for it. She knew that the king could take over the property of a criminal who was condemned to death. That would be a legal way of taking the land from Naboth. But how could Naboth be condemned to death? A serious crime had to be witnessed by two people. That was the law.

Jezebel thought about it until she formed a plan. She wrote a letter, sealed it with the king's seal, and sent copies to the leaders of Naboth's hometown.

The leaders who received the letters obeyed Jezebel's orders. They did exactly as she commanded. They called the people together and

brought Naboth before them. Then they called in a couple of rascals whom they had paid.

The two rascals said, "Naboth has cursed God and the king!"

The people decided that Naboth was guilty. They sentenced him to death by stoning.

The town leaders sent word to Jezebel, and she told Ahab the news. "Now get up!" she said. "Go take Naboth's vineyard, for he's not alive anymore. He's dead."

Ahab rose from his couch and rode down to Naboth's vineyard in Jezreel. With him were his two chariot captains, Jehu and Bidkar.

Just as he arrived at Naboth's vineyard, Ahab met Elijah.

"So!" said Ahab. "You've found me out, my enemy!"

"Yes," answered Elijah. "I've found you out. The Lord has sent me to give you a message. He says, first you committed murder, and now you're stealing property. Therefore, nobody in your family will receive a decent burial. All the men in your family will be swept away like garbage, like the families of Jeroboam and Baasha.

"And in the same place where the dogs licked the blood of Naboth, they'll lick your blood. Because Jezebel has influenced you, she'll be punished, too. The dogs of the city will eat her body in Jezreel."

Ahab was so shocked, he went right home. He put on plain rough clothing called sackcloth and mourned for his sins. He refused to eat. He even slept in the sackcloth. He walked through his palace slowly and quietly, praying to the Lord God for mercy.

The Lord heard Ahab's prayers. He said to Elijah, "Have you seen how Ahab has humbled himself before me? Because of this, I won't bring the disaster in his lifetime. I'll punish his family in the lifetime of his son."

16

The Lying Prophets

1 Kings 22; 2 Chronicles 17—18

DURING Ahab's reign the kingdom of Israel and the kingdom of Judah were at peace with each other. Ahab made an alliance with Jehoshaphat, the son of Asa. He gave his daughter Athaliah in marriage to Jehoshaphat's son Jehoram.

Ahab decided to use this alliance to help him against his old enemy, the Arameans. His alliance with King Ben-Hadad II had fallen apart, because Ben-Hadad refused to return the city of Ramoth in Gilead. Ahab was determined to attack the Arameans at Ramoth and win back the city.

He invited Jehoshaphat to visit him at his capital in Samaria. He gave a great feast in Jehoshaphat's honor, and then he said, "The city of Ramoth belongs to us, but we haven't done anything to take it. Jehoshaphat, will you come with me to fight the Arameans?"

"I'm as ready as you are," answered Jehoshaphat. "My men are as ready as your men, and my horses are as ready as your horses."

Jehoshaphat was not an idol worshiper. He served the Lord God and obeyed his commandments, always trying to follow the Lord's teachings. So he said to Ahab, "Please, before we do anything, let's first consult the Lord."

Ahab called together four hundred prophets who were loyal to him. They came to the open place by the city gate, where the two kings were sitting on their thrones, dressed in their royal robes.

"Should I march to Ramoth to attack the Arameans?" Ahab asked the prophets.

"March!" they answered. "The Lord will give you the victory!"

But Jehoshaphat wasn't satisfied. "Aren't there any other prophets?" he asked.

"Well," said Ahab, "there's one more, a fellow named Micaiah. But he never tells me anything good. He's always saying terrible things about me. I hate him!"

"Don't say that!" warned Jehoshaphat.

To please his ally Jehoshaphat, Ahab sent a servant to fetch Micaiah. Then he went back to listening to the four hundred loyal prophets.

One of them, a man named Zedekiah, had made iron horns to impress the king with his prophecy. He held them up and said, "See these horns! You'll be as strong as they are. You'll gore the Arameans like a wild ox, until you completely destroy them."

All the other prophets said the same thing. "You'll win," they said to Ahab. "March to Ramoth, and the Lord will give you victory. He'll put the Arameans in your power."

Just then Ahab's servant arrived with the prophet Micaiah. "See," he said to Micaiah, "all those prophets are prophesying victory for the king. If you know what's good for you, you'll do the same thing!"

"As the Lord lives," answered Micaiah, "I'll say what the Lord tells me to say."

Then Micaiah went and stood in front of King Ahab.

"Micaiah," said Ahab, "Should Jehoshaphat and I march to Ramoth?"

"Certainly," answered Micaiah. "You'll win. March to Ramoth, and the Lord will put the city in your power."

"Stop mocking me!" ordered Ahab. "Just tell us what the Lord has said to you."

"I have seen a vision," said Micaiah.

"I saw all Israel scattered on the mountains,
like sheep without a shepherd.
And I heard the Lord say, 'They have no master;
let them go home in peace.'"

When he heard Micaiah's prophecy, Ahab turned to Jehoshaphat and said, "Didn't I tell you this fellow wouldn't prophesy anything good for me?"

"Listen!" cried Micaiah. "Hear the word of the Lord. I have seen another vision.

"I saw the Lord seated on his heavenly throne with all the angels standing beside him. And the Lord said, 'Who will trick Ahab into marching to his death at Ramoth?'

"A spirit came forward and stood before the Lord and said, 'I will go. I'll be a lying spirit in the mouths of all of Ahab's loyal prophets.'

"Then the Lord said, 'Go, you'll succeed in tricking Ahab.'

"And this is what happened. The Lord himself has prophesied against you! He has put a lying spirit into the mouths of all your prophets."

The other prophets were furious. Zedekiah went up to Micaiah and slapped him on the cheek. "Since when did the spirit of the Lord leave me to speak through you?" he shouted.

"Someday you'll find out," answered Micaiah, "and that day you'll run away and hide."

"Seize Micaiah!" cried Ahab. "Arrest him and throw him into prison! Give him nothing but bread and water until I return in victory."

As they led Micaiah away, he looked at Ahab and said, "If you return in victory, then the Lord has not spoken through me."

Then King Ahab of Israel and King Jehoshaphat of Judah led their combined armies across the Jordan River into the mountains of Gilead. As they rode near the city of Ramoth, Ahab began to worry about Micaiah's prophecy. He said to Jehoshaphat, "I'm going to disguise myself when we go into battle. I'll dress like an ordinary soldier. But you wear your royal robes."

Before the battle King Ben-Hadad told his chariot captains not to attack anyone except the king of Israel. When they saw Jehoshaphat in his royal robes, they cried, "Look! There's the king of Israel."

They wheeled their chariots around and drove toward Jehoshaphat. Just as they were about to kill him, he cried out, and they realized that he was the king of Judah, not the king of Israel.

But someone else attacked Ahab. An Aramean bowman happened to shoot an arrow toward an ordinary-looking soldier. It was Ahab in disguise, and the arrow pierced his skin at an open place between two pieces of armor.

"Help!" he cried to his driver. "I'm wounded! Turn around and get me out of the battle so I can lie down."

But the battle was so fierce, the chariot driver couldn't turn around. Ahab stayed propped up in his chariot all afternoon, bleeding from his wound. The blood flowed down and covered the bottom of his chariot. At sunset, Ahab died.

The news of their king's death spread rapidly through the Israelite army. "We have no master!" the soldiers cried. "Let's go home!"

And all Israel scattered on the mountains, like sheep without a shepherd.

17

An Army That Didn't Fight and Ships That Didn't Sail

1 Kings 22; 2 Chronicles 19—20

KING Jehoshaphat of Judah left Ramoth and returned home to Jerusalem. On his way he met a prophet named Jehu.

Jehu said to him, "The Lord is displeased with you for making an alliance with Ahab. Should you love those who hate the Lord? But the Lord is glad that you are removing the idols from Judah."

Jehoshaphat had been encouraging his people to turn away from idols and to worship the Lord. When he arrived home, he appointed judges and told them, "Remember, when you decide cases you're not judging for human beings, but for the Lord. He'll be with you as you make your decisions. Be honest and fair."

Jehoshaphat himself went all over his kingdom, teaching the people about the ways of the Lord.

Then one day a messenger arrived at Jehoshaphat's palace with frightening news. A great army was headed straight for Jerusalem. The Moabites, the Ammonites, and the Edomites, who lived on the other side of the Salt Sea, were on their way to attack Judah.

Jehoshaphat told the people to fast and to pray. He invited them to come to the temple in Jerusalem for a special service to ask the Lord for help.

Men, women, and children—even the youngest—came from all over the kingdom of Judah. They gathered in front of the temple and prayed to the Lord.

Jehoshaphat stood in front of the great bronze pillars and spoke to the people. Then he prayed, "Lord God, ruler of heaven and earth, we cry out to you! We're afraid, and we don't know what to do. A great army is coming toward us! Lord, we're depending on you to save us."

As the king and the people prayed, the spirit of the Lord came over a man in the crowd. He was a Levite named Jehaziel.

"People of Judah!" cried Jehaziel. "The Lord

says, don't be afraid of this great army, for the battle doesn't depend on you, but on God. March out against them tomorrow. When you meet the enemy, take up your positions, but don't fight. Stand still and wait to see how the Lord will save you."

Jehoshaphat and the people bowed down and thanked the Lord for sending them Jehaziel's message. The temple singers praised the Lord with all their might.

Early the next morning the men of Judah went out to meet the enemy. As they were leaving the city, Jehoshaphat said to them, "Put your trust in the Lord your God, and you'll be safe. Believe his prophets, and you'll succeed."

Jehoshaphat told the temple singers to march in front of the army. As they marched, they sang,

"Praise to the Lord,
for he is good;
And his mercy is everlasting!"

Their song was so loud, it reached the ears of the enemy soldiers who were coming toward them. They panicked, and the Ammonites and the Moabites attacked the Edomites. Then they turned around and attacked each other. The three armies completely wiped each other out.

Some of the men of Judah found a place looking out over the wilderness. They climbed up and saw the whole army of Ammonites, Edomites, and Moabites lying on the ground.

Jehoshaphat and his men went out and looted the enemy army. They found so much valuable equipment, it took them three days to gather it all.

Then Jehoshaphat led them back to Jerusalem, rejoicing and praising God.

For the rest of Jehoshaphat's life, the Lord gave peace to the kingdom of Judah. Jehoshaphat was faithful to the Lord, but one time he did something wrong, and he was punished.

Jehu the prophet had warned Jehoshaphat not to make alliances with those who hated the Lord. But he made one with Ahaziah, the son of Ahab. Ahaziah was now the king of Israel, and he was as wicked as his father.

Jehoshaphat wanted Ahaziah to help him build

ships at Ezion-geber. He planned to send them across the sea for gold and other treasures.

While the ships were being built, a prophet named Eliezer came to Jehoshaphat and said, "The Lord is going to destroy your ships because you made an alliance with Ahaziah."

Eliezar's words came true. The Lord caused the great ships to wreck in port before they ever sailed.

Elijah and the Messengers

2 Kings 1

JEHOSHAPHAT understood that the destruction of the great sailing ships was a punishment from the Lord. But Ahaziah ignored the Lord.

One day Ahaziah, king of Israel, fell from the balcony of his palace in Samaria. He was so badly injured, he thought he might die. He sent some messengers to consult the god of Ekron, Baalzebul. (The worshipers of the Lord called this Philistine god Baalzebub, Baal of the Flies, instead of Baalzebul, Baal the Prince.)

Then the Lord sent a messenger to Elijah. An angel came and said to him, "Go out and meet Ahaziah's messengers and say to them, 'Isn't there a God in Israel? Why are you going to consult Baalzebub, the god of Ekron? You'll never leave this bed alive. You'll die from your injuries!"

Elijah did as the angel commanded. He went out to meet Ahaziah's messengers, who turned right around and went back to Samaria.

"Why have you come back?" Ahaziah asked them.

They explained, "A man came to meet us," and they told him what Elijah had said.

"Tell me," said Ahaziah. "What did this man look like?"

"He was wearing a hairy mantle and a leather loincloth."

"Elijah! That was Elijah!" screamed Ahaziah, and he ordered a captain to take fifty soldiers and go get the prophet.

The captain and his men found Elijah sitting on top of a hill. The captain went up to him and said, "Man of God, the king says, 'Come down.'"

"If I am a man of God," said Elijah, "may fire come down from heaven and destroy you and your soldiers."

Fire came down from heaven and struck the captain and his fifty men.

Then King Ahaziah sent another officer with another fifty soldiers. The second captain went up to Elijah and said, "Man of God, the king has ordered you to come down at once!"

"If I am a man of God," said Elijah, "may fire come down from heaven and destroy you and your soldiers."

Fire came down from heaven and destroyed the captain and his fifty men.

Then King Ahaziah sent a third captain and another fifty men. The third captain went up to Elijah and fell on his knees in front of him. "Man of God," he begged, "may my life and the lives of

these fifty men have some value in your eyes. Fire has come down from heaven and struck two captains and a hundred men. Have mercy on me!"

Then the angel of the Lord said to Elijah, "Go down with him. Don't be afraid."

Elijah got up and went with the third captain to see the king. When he arrived at the palace, he said to Ahaziah, "Because you sent messengers to consult Baalzebub, you'll never leave this bed alive. You'll die of your injuries."

Elijah's prophecy came true. Ahaziah never left his bed alive, for he died of his injuries.

Because Ahaziah had no son, his brother Joram became king. At about the same time, Jehoshaphat died, and his son Jehoram became king of Judah. Jehoram was married to Athaliah, the sister of Joram. So the king of Israel was a son of Ahab and the king of Judah was married to a daughter of Ahab.

Stories About Elisha

The Chariot of Fire

2 Kings 2

IT was time for the Lord to take Elijah away. After many years of serving as the Lord's prophet, he was going to heaven. His work wasn't finished, but Elisha would serve as the Lord's prophet after him.

Elijah left Gilgal, a town just a few miles north of Bethel, where he had been staying. Elisha started to go along, but Elijah said, "Please stay here. The Lord is only sending me to Bethel."

"As the Lord lives and as you live," answered Elisha, "I won't leave you!"

They went down to Bethel together. There they met some members of the community of prophets who lived at Bethel.

The prophets asked Elisha, "Do you know that the Lord is going to take your master away from you today?"

"Yes, I know. But don't talk about it."

Then Elijah said to Elisha, "Stay here. The Lord is only sending me to Jericho."

"As the Lord lives and as you live," answered Elisha, "I won't leave you!"

They went up to Jericho together. There they met some members of the community of prophets who lived at Jericho.

The prophets came to Elisha and asked, "Do you know that the Lord is going to take your master away from you today?"

"Yes, I know. But don't say anything."

Then Elijah said to Elisha, "Stay here. The Lord is only sending me to the Jordan River."

"As the Lord lives and as you live," answered Elisha, "I won't leave you!"

They went on to the river together, with fifty of the prophets following them. When they reached the bank of the river, they stopped, and the fifty prophets stopped a little way behind them.

Elijah took off his mantle, rolled it up, and struck the river with it. The water divided in two, and Elijah and Elisha crossed over to the other side with dry feet.

Then Elijah said to Elisha, "Tell me what you want me to do for you before I'm taken away."

Elisha answered, "I want your spirit to come over me. I want to inherit from you as the oldest son inherits from his father."

"That's not up to me," said Elijah. "But if you see me while I'm being taken away, you'll receive what you have asked for."

Then the two men walked on together, speaking of many things.

Suddenly Elisha saw a chariot of fire in the sky, and horses of fire appeared between him and Elijah. A great whirlwind picked Elijah up and carried him to heaven.

"My father! My father!" cried Elisha as Elijah disappeared. "You're the strength of Israel! You're our horses and chariots!"

And then Elijah was gone from his sight.

Elisha reached down and picked Elijah's mantle up from the ground. He carried it back to the river and struck the water with it. "Where is the Lord, the God of Elijah?" he cried.

He struck the water again, and this time it divided in two, and Elisha crossed over to the other side with dry feet.

The fifty prophets were waiting for him on the other side of the river. They hadn't seen Elijah while he was being taken away, but they could tell that there was something different about Elisha now.

"The spirit of Elijah has come upon Elisha!"

they said, and they bowed down before him.

Then they said, "There are fifty of us, all strong men. Let us go look for your master. Perhaps the Lord has left him on a mountaintop, or in a valley."

"No," said Elisha. "Don't bother looking for him."

They insisted, so he let them go and search. They looked for three days, and then they returned. They could find no trace of Elijah.

"Didn't I tell you?" said Elisha. He knew that Elijah was no longer in this world.

20

Some Miracles of Elisha

2 Kings 4

ELISHA stayed a while in the city of Jericho and lived with the community of prophets there. One day the wife of one of the prophets came to him and said, "Sir, my husband is dead. You know how much he loved the Lord! Now a man has come to collect a debt my husband owed, and I'm too poor to pay him. He'll take my sons as slaves to pay the debt if someone doesn't help me!"

"I want to help you," answered Elisha. "Tell me, what do you have in your house?"

"Nothing at all except a little pot of olive oil."

"Go to your neighbors and borrow as many empty pots and jars as you can. Then you and your sons go home and close the door and fill all the jars with oil."

The woman did as Elisha said. She borrowed pots and jars from her neighbors and took them home. Her sons passed the jars and she poured the oil into them. When all the jars were full, the woman said, "Pass me another."

"There aren't any more," said one of her sons.

At that moment the oil stopped flowing.

The woman returned to Elisha and told him what had happened.

"Go, sell the oil," he said. "It will pay all that you owe, and you'll have enough left over to support your family."

After this miracle and others, Elisha left Jericho to visit communities of prophets in other cities and towns. In his travels he often passed through the town of Shunem. One day a noblewoman invited him to come to her house to eat. In the months that followed, every time Elisha passed through Shunem, he stopped at her home for a meal.

One day the woman said to her husband, "I'm sure this man is a holy man of God. Let's build a small room for him on the roof. We can furnish it with a bed, a table, a chair, and an oil lamp, and he can rest here whenever he passes through."

Her husband agreed, and they built the room

for Elisha. He stayed there with his servant, Gehazi, whenever he passed through Shunem.

One day while Elisha was resting in the up-stairs room, he said to Gehazi, "Call the Shunemite lady and ask her what I can do for her. She has been so kind to me—perhaps I could speak to someone for her, to do her a favor."

Gehazi gave the woman the message.

"I have all I need right here among my own people," she answered.

"Well," said Elisha, "then how can I repay her for everything she has done for me?"

Gehazi said, "The woman has no son, and her husband is an old man."

"Tell her to come here," said Elisha.

The woman came and stood at the entrance of Elisha's room.

He said to her, "This time next year you will have a son."

"Don't make fun of me, sir!" she said. "How could I have a child. It couldn't happen."

About a year later, just as Elisha had promised, the Shunemite lady had a son.

One morning a few years later the little boy went out with his father to a field where reapers were gathering the fall harvest. Suddenly the boy screamed, "Oh, my head! My head hurts!"

The father said to a servant, "Carry the boy to his mother."

The servant took the boy to his mother, and she held him in her arms all morning. At noon he died.

The Shunemite lady didn't tell her husband what had happened. She carried the little boy up to Elisha's room, laid him on the bed, and went out, shutting the door behind her.

"I'm going out," she said to her husband. "Tell the servant to bring the donkey, so I can hurry to see Elisha."

"Why are you going to see Elisha today?" he asked. "It's not a feast day or a holy day."

"Never mind. I'll be right back."

She got on the donkey and went as fast as she could to Mount Carmel, where Elisha was staying.

He saw her coming while she was still a long way off. "Look!" he said to Gehazi. "Here comes the Shunemite lady. Run to meet her and ask if she and her family are well."

Gehazi hurried off to meet the woman, but when he spoke to her, she wouldn't answer. She went straight up to Elisha and bowed down before him, holding on to his feet.

Gehazi tried to push her away, but Elisha said, "Leave her alone. Don't you see she's upset? Something's the matter, but the Lord hasn't revealed to me what it is."

Then the woman said, "Did I ask you for a son? Didn't I tell you not to make fun of me!"

Elisha turned to Gehazi and ordered, "Hurry! Take my walking stick and go to Shunem at once. Don't stop to greet anyone, and don't answer if anyone greets you. Go straight to her house and hold my rod over the little boy's face."

After Gehazi left, Elisha told the woman to go home.

She answered, "As the Lord lives and as you live, I won't leave you!"

Then Elisha went with her to Shunem. On the way they met Gehazi. He had laid Elisha's rod over the little boy's face, but nothing had happened.

"The child didn't wake up," he said. "There was no sound, no sign of life."

When Elisha arrived at Shunem, he found the boy lying on the bed, dead. Elisha went into the room, closed the door, and prayed to the Lord. Then he climbed up onto the bed and lay over the boy, with his mouth on the boy's mouth, his eyes on the boy's eyes, and his hands on the boy's hands. As Elisha lay stretched out over the child, the child's body began to grow warm.

Elisha got up and walked back and forth in the room. Then he climbed up onto the bed again and stretched out over the boy seven times.

The little boy sneezed and opened his eyes.

Elisha called Gehazi and told him to bring the Shunemite woman upstairs. When she arrived, he said to her, "Pick up your son."

She came and fell at Elisha's feet. Then she got up and took her son and went out.

Elisha did many other wonderful works, because the spirit of the Lord, which had given power to Elijah, was now on him.

One time when he was teaching a large group of young prophets, a man came to Elisha with twenty small loaves of barley bread and some fresh fruit.

"Give the food to these people to eat," Elisha told his servant.

"How can I serve such a small amount to a hundred men?" asked the servant.

"Give it to the people," said Elisha. "For the Lord says they will eat and have some left over."

He passed out the bread and the fruit, and a hundred men ate. They all had enough, and there was some left over, as the Lord had said.

21

Elisha Finds Hazael

2 Kings 8; 2 Chronicles 21—22

THE news of Elisha's miracles spread throughout Israel and to other nations, too. Even Ben-Hadad II, king of the Arameans, heard about Elisha's power.

One day Ben-Hadad became ill. When he found out that Elisha happened to be in Damascus, he called one of his servants and said, "Elisha has come all the way from Israel. Go to him, give him a gift, and ask him to pray to the Lord to find out whether I'm going to get well."

This official was a man named Hazael. He

loaded forty camels with the best products of Damascus and took them to Elisha.

"Ben-Hadad sent me," he explained. "He wants you to find out if he's going to recover from his illness."

Elisha wasn't surprised. The Lord had sent him to Damascus to find Hazael. Some years earlier the Lord had told Elijah to call three men. Elisha was the first man, and now he was calling the other two, first Hazael and then Jehu. The Lord was about to punish the idol worshipers of Israel. He was going to use Hazael against them.

Elisha said to Hazael, "You can tell King Ben-Hadad that he'll recover, but the Lord has already told me that he will die."

Then Elisha stared hard at Hazael. Suddenly he began to cry.

"Why are you crying, my lord?" asked Hazael.

Elisha answered, "I see what harm you're going to do to the people of Israel. You're going to burn down their fortress cities and massacre their young men, women, and tiny children."

"That's not possible," said Hazael. "How could I do such things? I'm not an important man. I have no more power than a dog!"

Elisha looked at Hazael and said, "The Lord has shown me that you're going to become the king of the Arameans."

Hazael left Elisha and went back to the palace.

"What did Elisha tell you?" asked Ben-Hadad.

Hazael answered, "He said you'd certainly

recover from your illness."

The next day Hazael took a blanket and soaked it in water and spread it over the sick king's face. Ben-Hadad died, and Hazael became king.

Hazael declared war on Israel by sending an army to attack the Israelite city of Ramoth in Gilead.

King Joram of Israel led his army to defend the city, and King Ahaziah of Judah joined him. Ahaziah was Joram's nephew. His father was Jehoram, son of Jehoshaphat, and his mother was Athaliah, daughter of Ahab.

Athaliah had been a bad influence on her hus-

band, the wicked king Jehoram. Now she was her son's closest adviser. She urged him to go to Ramoth to help her brother, King Joram.

During the battle at Ramoth, Joram was wounded by an enemy arrow. He returned to his palace at Jezreel to rest and recover. Athaliah advised Ahaziah to visit him. While the two kings were at Jezreel, disaster struck the royal families of Israel and Judah. The time had come for the Lord to wipe out the family of Ahab and Jezebel.

22

Jehu's Revolt

2 Kings 9

WHEN Joram was wounded at Ramoth, Elisha knew it was time to call the third man the Lord had chosen to punish the idol worshipers. He sent for one of the young prophets and said to him, "Go to Ramoth, to the place where the army officers are meeting. Take this small jar of olive oil with you. Find Commander Jehu and take him to a private room, away from the other officers. Then anoint him with this oil and tell him that the Lord says, 'I have anointed you as king over Israel.' Then open the door and get out of there as fast as you can."

The young prophet did as Elisha said. He went to Ramoth and found the senior army officers meeting together. He went up to them and said, "I have a message for you, commander."

"For which one of us?" asked Jehu,

"For you, sir."

Jehu got up and followed the young prophet into a private room. The prophet poured the oil on Jehu's head and said, "The Lord says, 'I have anointed you as king over Israel.' "

Then the young prophet opened the door and ran away. Jehu returned to his companions.

"Is everything all right?" they asked. "What did that crazy fellow want with you?"

"You know what those prophets are like," he answered.

"Come on," they said, "tell us what he said!"

"Well—he told me that the Lord has anointed me as king over Israel."

The other officers immediately took off their cloaks and spread them out for Jehu to stand on. This was a sign that they were ready to serve him. Then they sounded the trumpet and shouted, "Jehu is king!"

Jehu said to them, "If you're going to be loyal to me, then don't let anyone leave this city to go to Jezreel and warn Joram."

Jehu got into his chariot and drove as fast as he could to Jezreel, where Joram was recovering from his wounds.

The watchman in the tower of Jezreel saw Jehu and his men as they approached. "I see some men riding up!" he shouted.

Joram thought the riders were bringing news from the battle at Ramoth. He said to a servant, "Send a horseman to ask if everything is all right."

The horseman rode out to meet Jehu. "The king wants to know if everything is all right," he said.

Jehu answered, "What business is that of yours? Follow me!"

Then the watchman in the tower reported, "The messenger has reached the chariots, but he's not coming back."

Joram sent out another horseman, who said to Jehu, "The king wants to know if everything is all right."

"That's none of your business," answered Jehu. "Follow me!"

"The second horseman isn't returning!" reported the watchman. "The driver of the first chariot reminds me of Jehu—he drives like a madman!"

"Harness my chariot!" ordered Joram.

King Joram of Israel and King Ahaziah of Judah rode out in their chariots to meet Jehu. They happened to reach him at the edge of the field that used to be Naboth's vineyard.

"Is everything all right?" asked Joram. He was worried about the war in Gilead.

"What a question!" answered Jehu. "How can

everything be all right when your mother, Queen Jezebel, continues her witchcraft and idol worship?"

Joram wheeled his chariot around, crying out, "Treason, Ahaziah!"

But it was too late. Jehu had already drawn his bow, and he shot an arrow into Joram's heart. Joram sank down to the bottom of his chariot, dead.

"Pick him up! shouted Jehu to his driver, Bidkar. "Throw Joram's body into Naboth's vineyard."

Then he said, "Bidkar, don't you remember when you and I drove chariot teams for Ahab, and the Lord warned Ahab that his son would be killed in this exact place?"

Then Jehu saw Ahaziah trying to escape. He chased after him, shouting, "Strike him down!"

Jehu's men wounded Ahaziah as he raced up the road in his chariot. Ahaziah kept on going until he reached the city of Megiddo, where he

died. His servants took his body back to Jerusalem for a decent burial.

Meanwhile, Joram's mother, Queen Jezebel, heard the news of Jehu's revolt. She prepared herself for the worst. She put on eye shadow and arranged her hair. Then she went and stood by a window and looked down at the street.

As soon as Jezebel saw Jehu come driving through the city gate toward the palace, she cried out, "Is everything all right, you Zimri! You assassin! Killer of kings!"

Jehu looked up at the window and called, "Who's on my side? Who?"

Two or three palace officials looked out at him.

"Throw her down!" he ordered.

They threw Jezebel out of the window. Some of her blood splattered on the wall and the horses where she fell. Then Jehu rode his chariot over her body.

Jehu went into the palace, sat down, and ate. When he was finished with his meal, he ordered, "Take that accursed woman and bury her! After all, she was the daughter of a king."

But when they went to bury Jezebel, all they could find of her were her skull and the bones of her hands and feet. The wild dogs of the city had eaten her body.

Jehu's servants came back and reported this to him, and he said, "That's what the Lord said would happen when he told Elijah about the shame that would come to the family of Ahab!"

23

Jehu Offers a Sacrifice

2 Kings 10; 2 Chronicles 22

JEHU was determined to wipe out the rest of the royal family. He knew that Joram's sons were living in Samaria, so he wrote a letter and sent copies to the nobles of the city.

The letter said, "You have Joram's children, his sons and nephews. You also have horses, chariots, weapons, and fortress cities. As soon as you receive this letter, choose the best of your master's sons and set him on his father's throne and fight to defend his family."

The nobles of Samaria were terrified. Was

Jehu testing them? Was he challenging them to civil war?

"How can we stand up to Jehu?" they asked each other. "King Joram of Israel and King Ahaziah of Judah were no match for him!"

They sent a messenger to Jehu, saying, "We're your loyal subjects. We'll do whatever you say. But we won't choose anyone to be king. You do what you think is best."

Jehu wrote them another letter, saying, "If you're for me, then bring the heads of Ahab's family to me at Jezreel by this time tomorrow."

The nobles of Samaria took Joram's sons and nephews and slaughtered all seventy of them. They put their heads in baskets and sent them to Jehu at Jezreel.

When a messenger reported this to Jehu, he said, "Put them in two heaps at the city gate until tomorrow morning."

The next morning Jehu went out to the gate and met the people. He said to them, "I'm the one who plotted against the king and killed him. You're not responsible for that. But I didn't murder these people. The Lord's prophecy through Elijah is coming true!"

Then Jehu hunted down all of Ahab's family he could find in Jezreel, and had all of them killed. He also found and executed all the officials, friends, and priests of the royal family.

Jehu then left Jezreel and went to Samaria. On the way he met Jehonadab, son of Rechab, coming to meet him. Jehonadab was the leader of a community of people who worshiped the Lord and lived in the wilderness, following a strict order of life.

"Are you with me?" asked Jehu.

"Yes," answered Jehonadab.

"Then give me your hand," said Jehu, and he brought Jehonadab up into his chariot. "Come with me and see how devoted I am to the Lord!"

They arrived in Samaria and hunted down all the members of Ahab's family they could find and killed them.

Then Jehu called the people of the city together and said to them, "Ahab served Baal a little, but Jehu will serve him a lot! Bring me all the prophets of Baal, and all his priests. Don't leave anyone out, for I'm going to offer a great sacrifice!"

Jehu proclaimed a special day of worship in honor of Baal. He sent messengers all over Israel to invite every Baal worshiper to come to the temple in Samaria.

When the worshipers of Baal arrived, they packed into the temple. There were so many, they completely filled the building from wall to wall.

Jehu and Jehonadab came into the temple to greet the people. Jehu said to them, "Make sure that no worshiper of the Lord is in here. I want only worshipers of Baal here today."

Then Jehu went outside and spoke to the

eighty men he had put on guard. "Come in now," he said. "The idol worshipers are waiting. Strike them all down. Don't let a single one get away!"

The guards entered the temple with their swords in their hands. They struck the prophets and priests and worshipers of Baal, killing every one of them.

Then they went to the inner room of the temple and pulled down the great figure of the god Baal. They took the idol outside and burned it. Next they smashed the great altar outside the temple and wrecked the temple building itself. They turned the temple of Baal into a public toilet.

Now that Ahab's family was wiped out and the idol worshipers were destroyed, Jehu was firmly in power as king of Israel. But Jehu didn't

obey the Lord with his whole heart. He followed the example of Jeroboam and used religion to increase his own power.

Then the Lord said to Jehu, "I will reward you for punishing the idol worshipers. I'll make your son king after you. But because you have led Israel into sin, your family will rule for only four generations. Then they will be wiped out, like the families of Jeroboam, Baasha, and Ahab."

During Jehu's lifetime the Lord began to reduce Israel's territory. He allowed Hazael to conquer Gilead. Jehu made an alliance with the Assyrians, a strong nation in the north who would someday cause Israel more trouble than the Arameans. But now Jehu thought the Assyrians would protect his kingdom against Hazael and the Arameans.

After a long reign, Jehu died and his son Jehoahaz became king.

24

The Little Prince Who Hid in the Temple

2 Kings 11—12; 2 Chronicles 22—24

WHEN King Ahaziah of Judah was killed by Jehu's men, Ahaziah's mother, Queen Athaliah, decided to take over the kingdom. She gave orders for the rest of the royal family of Judah to be killed, so no one could challenge her right to the throne.

All of Ahaziah's sons were killed except a baby named Joash. His aunt Jehosheba, a half sister of Ahaziah, saved him. She took Joash and his nurse and hid them in one of the rooms of the temple. Jehosheba's husband, Jehoiada, was the high priest. He taught little Joash about the Lord and prepared him to be king.

For the next six years Queen Athaliah ruled Judah and little Joash hid in the temple.

When Joash was seven years old, Jehoiada, the high priest, plotted to make him king. He called the army officers together and told them his plan. Then he sent them throughout the land to bring the leaders of Judah to Jerusalem.

When they arrived, Jehoiada brought little Joash out to them and said, "Here is our king, the son of Ahaziah!"

The next Sabbath day, while the people were going up to the temple to worship, Jehoiada ordered the soldiers and temple guards to take positions around the building. Some surrounded the temple and others guarded little Joash. They all had their swords ready in their hands.

Then Jehoiada led Joash out to the front of the temple. He placed the crown on his head and anointed the boy as king of Judah. The people clapped and shouted, "God save the king!"

When Queen Athaliah heard the shouting, she hurried from her palace up the hill to the temple. But when she arrived, she wasn't able to get past the guards who were standing around the building with their swords and shields. Over the tops of the heads of the crowd she could see the little boy with the crown on his head. He was standing with Jehoiada, the high priest, beside the great bronze pillars in front of the temple.

"Treason! Treason!" cried Athaliah.

"Take her out!" ordered Jehoiada. "Guard her carefully so no one can rescue her."

The soldiers led Athaliah away. They walked her past the line of armed men and away from the temple area, to put her to death.

Then Jehoiada spoke to the people. He reminded them that the Lord was their God. The people and the king agreed to serve the Lord, and the people promised to obey God and the king. The king promised to rule Judah according to the Lord's teachings.

Jehoiada led Joash and the people from the temple to the palace, and the new king took his seat on the throne of David.

Joash was king of Judah for forty years. In the beginning of his reign he obeyed the Lord and ruled wisely. Jehoiada the high priest gave the young king good advice. The people pulled down the idols and altars which Athaliah had built, and all of Judah returned to the Lord.

Athaliah had neglected and damaged the temple, so Joash decided to repair it. Jehoiada asked all the people to help by bringing silver to pay for the repairs.

As long as Jehoiada lived, Joash ruled Judah according to the teachings of the Lord. But when Jehoiada died, Joash turned to other people for advice. He and the people of Judah began to ignore the teachings of the Lord, and soon they were worshiping idols again.

The Lord sent prophets to warn them, but they refused to listen. One of these prophets was Zechariah, the son of Jehoiada. He came into the courtyard of the temple one day to speak to the king and the people. He was filled with the spirit of the Lord.

"Listen!" shouted Zechariah. "The Lord God wants to know why you have disobeyed his commandments. You're bringing disaster on yourselves. Remember—when you abandon the Lord, he abandons you."

Joash's advisers encouraged him to put Zechariah to death. He joined them in a plot against the prophet, even though Zechariah was the son of his good friend and teacher, Jehoiada. He ordered the people to stone Zechariah to death, right there in the courtyard of the temple.

As Zechariah was dying, he called out, "May the Lord see what you're doing and punish you for it!"

The very next year the Lord sent Hazael, king of Damascus, to invade Judah with a small army. Hazael captured the city of Gath and killed many leaders of Judah. He was about to attack Jerusalem, but Joash gave him some gold from the treasury and Hazael pulled back his army and returned home.

Joash was so upset, he became ill and went to bed. Two of his officials plotted against him. They murdered him in revenge for the murder of Zechariah.

Joash's son Amaziah became the next king of Judah.

25

How Naaman Was Healed

2 Kings 5

NAAMAN was an important man. He was a commander in the Aramean army, greatly respected by his master the king. But Naaman suffered from a terrible skin disease called leprosy. He could win great victories in battle, but he was helpless against the disease.

In the house of this important person lived a little servant girl. She had been captured by the Arameans in one of their raids against Israel, and now she waited on Naaman's wife.

One day the little girl said to her mistress, "I

wish my master would go to the prophet in Samaria. He would cure Naaman's leprosy."

When Naaman heard this, he told the king what the little girl had said.

"Go!" said the king. "I'll write a letter to the king of Israel."

Naaman took the letter and set out for Israel. He and his servants rode in chariots, bringing gifts of six thousand pieces of gold, thirty thousand pieces of silver, and ten beautiful robes.

When he arrived in Samaria, Naaman went to the king of Israel and gave him the letter from the king of Damascus. The letter said, "I'm sending my commander Naaman to you. I want you to cure him of his leprosy."

The king of Israel was frightened. "I'm not a god!" he said. "I have no power over life or death. Why does the king of Damascus ask me to cure this man? He's just looking for an excuse to start a war!"

Elisha heard about what was happening, and he sent a message to the king of Israel, saying, "Why are you so upset? Send Naaman to me, and he'll find out that there is a prophet in Israel."

The king sent Naaman to Elisha, and Naaman went to Elisha's house with all his servants and horses and chariots.

But instead of coming out to meet his important guest, Elisha sent a servant to say, "Go wash yourself seven times in the Jordan River, and your skin will be made clean."

Naaman wasn't used to such treatment. He expected more honor and respect. He said to one of his servants, "I was sure the man would come out and meet me and pray to his God and wave his hand over the diseased place and cure me. Surely, the rivers of Damascus are better than any river in Israel. I could have stayed at home and washed in them."

He was so angry, he started to leave.

"Sir," said one of Naaman's servants, "if the prophet had told you to do something difficult, you'd do it, wouldn't you? Why don't you just go wash yourself as he says and be cured?"

Naaman listened to his servant's advice. He went down to the Jordan River and dipped

himself into the water seven times. When he came out of the water, his skin was as smooth as the skin of a little child. He was completely cured.

Naaman hurried back to Elisha's house, and this time the prophet came out to meet him.

Naaman said, "Now I know there is no God in all the earth except in Israel! Please, sir, accept a gift from me."

"No," answered Elisha. "As the Lord lives, I won't accept a thing."

Naaman insisted, but Elisha refused.

Naaman didn't feel important anymore, so he said to Elisha, "If you won't accept my gift, then please let me have two muleloads of earth to take home with me." He wanted to build an altar to the Lord in Damascus with dirt from Israel.

He explained, "From now on I won't offer sacrifices to any god except the Lord. When I go with my master the king to the temple of his god Rimmon and bow down before the idol, I hope the Lord will forgive me."

"Go in peace," said Elisha.

A few minutes later Elisha's servant Gehazi ran after Naaman's chariot. Gehazi had been thinking, "Elisha has let this Aramean get away without taking anything from him. Well, I'll get something for myself."

When Naaman saw Gehazi, he got down from his chariot and asked, "Is everything all right?"

"Yes," answered Gehazi. "My master has sent

me to tell you that two of the servants of the prophets have just arrived. He would like you to give them three thousand pieces of silver."

"Here," said Naaman, "Take six thousand pieces." He put the silver pieces into two bags, tied them, and handed them to a pair of his servants. The servants carried the bags back toward Elisha's house. Before they could get there, Gehazi took the bags of silver from them and hid them. Then he went on to Elisha's house.

"Where have you been, Gehazi?" asked Elisha.

"Nowhere, sir."

"That's not true, Gehazi. I could see you in my mind when a certain man got down from his chariot to greet you. Have you taken silver to buy yourself orchards and olive groves, vineyards and sheep and oxen and servants? Oh, Gehazi. You'll be punished for this. You'll suffer from the leprosy that left Naaman!"

And when Gehazi went out, he found leprosy on his skin.

26

Elisha Captures Some Raiders

2 Kings 13; 6

THE Lord was letting the Arameans defeat Israel because Jehu's son Jehoahaz was worshiping idols. King Hazael of Damascus and his son Ben-Hadad III attacked until Israel had only a small army of fifty horsemen, ten chariots, and ten units of foot soldiers. All the rest were trampled down like dust beneath the feet of the Arameans.

But the Lord didn't completely turn his people over to the power of their enemies. He gave Elisha power to defeat them. Elisha was more valuable to Israel than all their horses and chariots. When the Arameans sent raiding parties over the border, Elisha told the king where they would strike, so the Israelites were ready for them when they came.

This upset the king of Aram so much, he said to his officers, "Which one of you is betraying us to the king of Israel?"

"None of us, my lord king," answered one of the officers. "Elisha tells the king of Israel everything you say, even the words you speak in the privacy of your bedroom!"

"Go find Elisha," ordered the king. "I'll send some men to capture him."

They discovered that Elisha was staying at Dothan, a town just outside of Samaria. They sent a band of armed men who arrived in the middle of the night and surrounded the town.

The next morning Elisha and his servant went outside and saw the Arameans and their horses and chariots all around the town.

"Oh, master!" cried the servant. "What will become of us?"

"Don't be afraid," said Elisha. "There are more on our side than on theirs."

Then Elisha prayed, "O Lord, open my servant's eyes so he can see what I see."

The servant looked up and saw the hillside covered with horses and chariots of fire.

The Arameans couldn't see the heavenly army protecting the prophet. They rode right toward him, expecting to take him prisoner.

Then Elisha prayed, "O Lord, strike these men so they can't see what they're looking at."

The Lord answered his prayer, and Elisha went up to the Arameans and said, "This isn't the town you're looking for. Follow me, and I'll lead you to the man you're hunting."

He guided the Arameans out of Dothan and into Samaria. As soon as they were inside the city, Elisha prayed, "O Lord, open their eyes so they can see where they are."

The Lord answered his prayer, and the Arameans realized that they were in the middle of

Samaria, with Israelite soldiers all around them.

"Should I kill them?" the king asked Elisha.

"No," he answered. "Don't kill the prisoners. Feed them and send them back to their king."

The king of Israel did as Elisha said. He gave the Aramean prisoners a great feast and then sent them back to Damascus.

After that, no more raiders bothered Israel.

27

What the Lepers Found Outside the Gates

2 Kings 6—7

A few years after Elisha captured the raiders, Ben-Hadad III led his whole army against Israel. He besieged Samaria, surrounding the city with his army and cutting it off from food and water, to force the people to surrender.

Inside Samaria, the people were dying of hunger and thirst. Food was so scarce that a few onions were selling for five pieces of silver.

Some of the people were going crazy with hunger. Finally, the king of Israel couldn't stand it any longer. He sent for Elisha, who was sitting in his house talking to some of the nobles of the city.

Just before the king's messengers arrived, Elisha said, "He's sending someone to cut off my head. Hold the door. The king himself is coming right behind them!"

While Elisha was still speaking, the king arrived. "I don't trust the Lord," he said to Elisha. "Why should I? He brought this misery on us."

Elisha answered, "Hear the word of the Lord. By this time tomorrow, food will be so plentiful in the streets of Samaria that twenty pounds of grain will be selling for one piece of silver."

"No," said one of the officials who was with the king. "That's impossible. It couldn't happen, not even if the Lord made windows in the sky!"

"You'll see it with your own eyes," said Elisha, "but you won't eat any of it because you have defied the Lord."

The next morning four lepers happened to be standing outside the gates of Samaria. Lepers weren't allowed inside the city because of their disease.

They were arguing among themselves.

"Why should we sit out here, waiting to starve to death?" asked one.

"Well," said another, "if we go into the city, we'll starve to death there."

The third leper said, "We'll certainly starve out here!"

"I have an idea," said the fourth one. "Come on,

147

let's go out to the Aramean camp. If they don't kill us, they might feed us. And if they kill us—well, we'd die anyway."

That night the four lepers went out in the dark to the place where the Aramean army was camped. They found the horses and donkeys tied up, but there were no people in the whole camp. They didn't hear a single human voice.

The lepers went into a tent and found it just as the Arameans had left it. They ate and drank what they found and took the silver and gold and robes and hid them.

Then they came back and went into another tent and did the same thing.

What had happened to the Arameans? Earlier that night the Lord had caused them to hear the sound of horses and chariots. They were sure that a great army was on the way to relieve Samaria, and they ran away in panic, leaving all their valuables behind them.

The lepers were stuffing themselves and having a good time until one of them said, "This isn't right. This is a day of good news, and we're keeping it to ourselves. If we wait until morning, someone else will come out here and discover what's going on, and we'll be in trouble. Let's go to the city right now and tell them the news!"

The four lepers walked back to Samaria. As they came near the gate of the city, they called out to the watchmen, "We went to the Aramean camp and found it empty."

The guards took the news to the palace.

"I don't believe it!" said the king. "Those Arameans are up to something. They know we're starving, and they're hiding somewhere in the countryside, just waiting for us to come out, so they can catch us."

One of the king's advisers said, "The people will die of starvation if they stay in the city. Why don't you send some horsemen to find out what's going on?"

The king followed this advice and sent out some horsemen. They found the camp deserted, just as the lepers had reported. Then they rode on to the Jordan River, where they found the Arameans' equipment scattered all along the road.

They returned to Samaria with the good news. The siege was over!

The people of the city rushed out to the Aramean camp to get food. They brought back so much that on that day twenty pounds of barley was sold in the streets of Samaria for one piece of silver.

The officer in command of the city gate was the same man who had gone to Elisha's house with the king the day before. He was the one who said God couldn't do such a miracle.

He saw it with his own eyes, but he didn't eat any of the food, for the people rushing through the gate trampled him to death.

Once more, Elisha's prophecy came true.

28

The Strength of Israel

2 Kings 13—14; 2 Chronicles 25

ONE day Elisha sent for Jehoash, king of Israel. He was the son of Jehoahaz, who was the son of Jehu. Elisha was now an old man, and he wanted to give the king one last message before he died.

"My father, my father," cried Jehoash. "You're the strength of Israel! You're our chariots and horsemen!"

"Get a bow and arrow," said Elisha. Then he said, "Draw the bow."

Jehoash lifted up his hand, and Elisha put his

hands over the king's, as a sign that his power was going to the king.

"Open the window toward the east," said Elisha.

Jehoash opened the window facing Damascus.

"The Lord's arrow of victory over the Arameans," cried Elisha. "You'll save Israel from them. You'll completely defeat them in battle!"

Then he said, "Take the arrow and shoot!"

Jehoash shot the arrow.

"Take the rest of the arrows."

Jehoash took them.

"Strike them on the ground."

Jehoash struck the arrows on the ground three times. Then he stopped.

"You should have struck the ground at least six times," said Elisha. "Then you would have completely destroyed the Arameans. You gave up too soon. For this reason, you'll win only three victories over them—one for each arrow. Someone else will destroy them."

A little while later Elisha died. Jehoash lived to fight the Arameans three times and win, as Elisha had prophesied.

When Jehoash died, his son Jeroboam II became king of Israel. Jeroboam completely destroyed the Arameans, so they never threatened Israel again.

In Judah, Joash's son Amaziah was followed by Amaziah's son Uzziah.

In the two hundred years from the time of Solomon to the time of Jeroboam II and Uzziah, many great kings ruled over Israel and Judah. But God showed his power especially in the wonderful works of his prophets, and he made their words come true.

Songs and
Sayings

29

Words of Wisdom

The Book of Proverbs

WHEN Solomon was king of Israel, he encouraged the scribes at his court to write histories and collect poems, stories, and wise sayings. Solomon himself wrote many wise sayings, or proverbs. Some of them were combined with other collections of writings to become the part of the Bible called the book of Proverbs.

Proverbs contains a type of writing called "Wisdom." Wisdom writing is found in several other books of the Bible, but Proverbs is the best-known of the Wisdom books.

The ancient Israelites loved all sorts of knowledge. They used proverbs and other wisdom writings in their homes and schools to teach boys and girls how to live.

At the beginning of the book, the king is advising his son. He says, "The first stage of knowledge is to honor the Lord. Then pay attention to the teaching of your father and mother. What you learn at home will keep you safe when you go out into the world. Listen to your teachers. Search for wisdom like buried treasure. When you find it, you'll learn about God, for he is the source of all wisdom.

"My son," says the king, "don't forget what your parents teach you. And remember—knowledge is not enough! Don't depend on your own intelligence. Don't become proud. Trust the Lord, honor him, and he will guide you. Give the Lord the first part of everything you earn. When the Lord corrects you, don't be upset, for he is like a father who disciplines the child he loves.

"Once I was a little child like you. I was my mother's darling. And my father used to tell me, 'Get wisdom! Get understanding!' "

In another section of Proverbs, wisdom is described as a wise woman. She stands by the city gate, calling out to the people.

"Learn the truth!" she cries. "Knowledge is more valuable than gold. Understanding is more precious than pearls. If you seek me, you will find me."

The wise woman, Wisdom, explains about herself, "It is wisdom that enables rulers to govern fairly. Through wisdom, the Lord created heaven and earth.

"The Lord created wisdom first, before he made anything else. I was born before the seas and mountains. I played by God's side while he designed the rivers and hills. And when he finished making the earth, I played in it. I was delighted with human beings!"

Another woman in Proverbs is the perfect housewife. In the last chapter of Proverbs, a long poem describes her as a hard worker and shrewd businesswoman. She rises early in the morning, while it is still dark, to begin her work. She buys a field, plants a vineyard, spins thread, weaves cloth, and sews a quilt. She sells her handiwork to provide for her family. She gives generously to the poor.

She is such a good manager, so strong and so wise, the leaders of the city respect her and her husband. Her husband and sons tell everyone how wonderful she is.

> Who can find a perfect wife?
> She is worth more than pearls.
>
> Charm is unreal, and beauty fades.
> The one to praise is the woman who is wise.

The main section of Proverbs is the collections of wise sayings. They are written in the form of

two-line poems. Here is a selection of twelve
from the hundreds you can find in the Bible.

A wise son is a joy to his father,
   but a foolish boy makes his mother sad.

Hatred starts arguments,
   but love covers up faults.

When God is pleased with you,
   he turns your enemies into friends.

Goodness makes a nation great,
  but sin disgraces the whole country.

Don't brag about tomorrow,
  for you don't even know what today will bring.

The Lord hates lying lips,
  but he loves those who tell the truth.

It's not good to eat a whole pot of honey,
  and it's bad to hear too many compliments.

When you give to the poor, you're lending to the
    Lord;
  he will repay you.

Grandparents are proud of their grandchildren,
  as children are proud of their parents.

Correction brings wisdom,
  but the child who has his own way will make
  his mother ashamed.

Let other people praise you;
  don't say nice things about yourself.

It's better to be wise than to be strong,
  for knowledge is power.

30

Songs of Love

The Song of Songs

ANOTHER book of the Bible associated with Solomon is the Song of Songs, also known as the Song of Solomon.

Solomon was famous for writing songs and for having many wives. The Song of Songs describes the powerful love between a young woman and a young man, perhaps Solomon and one of his wives.

Such love is one of God's greatest gifts. It is like the love between God and his people.

Here is a selection from the Song of Songs (which means "the best song").

Like a flower among thorns,
　　so is my darling among girls.

Like the apple in the wildwood,
　　so is my love among boys.

I am black and beautiful,
　　as black as the tents in the desert.

I am the rose of Sharon,
　　the lily of the valley.

I hear my beloved—
　　here he comes,

　　　leaping on the mountains,
　　　　jumping over the hills!

He is like a gazelle,
　　a strong and graceful deer.

He calls to me,
　　"Rise up, my darling,

　　　for the winter is past,
　　　　the rain is gone,

　　　　　the flowers are blooming—
　　　　　　spring is here!

Rise up, my darling;
　　come with me, my beloved!"

Show me your face;
　　let me hear your voice,

For your voice is sweet,
   and your face is beautiful.

You are completely beautiful, my love;
   you are perfect.

No river can drown our love;
   no water can put out its flames.

Love is as fierce as the underworld;
   love is as powerful as death!

THE WORLD OF SOLOMON, ELIJAH, AND ELISHA

Sidon

▲ Mount Lebanon

• Damascus

ARAM (SYRIA)

Zarephath

• Dan

PHOENICIA

Tyre

⌐ Mount Carmel

Cherith Valley

GILEAD

• Ramoth-gilead

Plain of Sharon

• Megiddo

Shunem

Jezreel

Dothan

Abel-Meholah

• Samaria

Great Western Sea (Mediterranean Sea)

I S R A E L

Jordan River

• Tirzah

• Shechem

• Shiloh

Gilgal •

• Bethel

Jericho

AMMON

• Gibeon

• Anathoth

PHILISTIA

• Ekron

• Jerusalem

JUDAH

Salt Sea

MOAB

• Beersheba

EGYPT

EDOM

to RED SEA

to ARABIA

KINGDOMS AND EMPIRES DURING THE TIME OF SOLOMON, ELIJAH, AND ELISHA

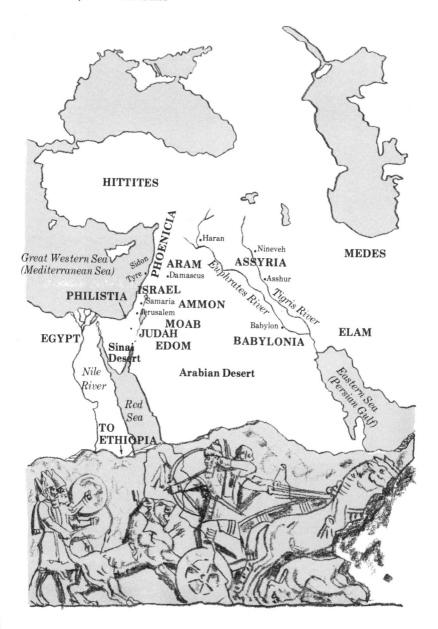

HITTITES

PHOENICIA

Haran

Nineveh

MEDES

Great Western Sea
(Mediterranean Sea)

Sidon

ARAM

ASSYRIA

Tyre

Damascus

Euphrates River

Asshur

Tigris River

PHILISTIA

ISRAEL

Samaria

AMMON

Jerusalem

MOAB

Babylon

EGYPT

JUDAH

BABYLONIA

ELAM

Sinai
Desert

EDOM

Nile
River

Arabian Desert

Eastern Sea
(Persian Gulf)

Red
Sea

TO
ETHIOPIA

Eve Bowers MacMaster graduated from the Pennsylvania State University and George Washington University. She also studied at Harvard University and Eastern Mennonite Seminary. She has taught in the Bible department at Eastern Mennonite College and in the history department at James Madison University, both located in Harrisonburg, Virginia.

Eve visited many of the places mentioned in the Bible while she was serving as a Peace Corps Volunteer in Turkey.

Eve and her husband, Richard, live near Harrisonburg, Virginia, with their children, Sam, Tom, and Sarah.